High-tech Geography

ICT in secondary schools

Compiled by Sheila King

Acknowledgements

The Geographical Association would like to thank David Hassell, Michael Rudd and Jayne Warburton as ICT editors, and the authors of the original articles. Special thanks also to David Hassell (BECTa) for his advice on the selection of material and his work on this book.

© the Geographical Association, 2000

This book is copyright under the Berne Convention. All rights are reserved. Apart from any unfair dealing for the purpose of private study, research, criticism or review, as permitted under the Copyright, Designs and Patents Act 1988, no part of this publication may be reproduced, stored in a retrieval system, or transmitted in any form or by any means, electronic, electrical, chemical, mechanical, optical, photocopying, recording or otherwise, without the prior permission of the copyright owner. Enquiries should be addressed to the Geographical Association. As a benefit of membership, the Association allows its members to reproduce material for their own internal school/departmental use, provided that the copyright is held by the GA. The views expressed in this publication are those of the author and do not necessarily represent those of the Geographical Association.

ISBN 1 899085 76 9
First published 2000
Impression number
10 9 8 7 6 5 4 3 2 1
Year 2003 2002 2001 2000

Published by the Geographical Association, 160 Solly Street, Sheffield S1 4BF. The Geographical Association is a registered charity: no. 313129

The Publications Officer of the GA would be happy to hear from other potential authors who have ideas for geography books. You may contact the Officer via the GA at the address above.

Design and typeset by ATG Design, Catalyst Creative Imaging
Printed and bound by Thanet Press

Contents

Introduction *Sheila King*	3

ICT IN THE CURRICULUM

1: Integrating ICT into schemes of work *David Gardner*	4
2: Planning for progression in IT activities *Helen Warner*	6
3: Assessing IT in geography *Keith Whiddon*	8
4: Using ICT in coursework *David Hassell*	10
5: ICT in geography-related GNVQ *David Hassell*	14

SOFTWARE AND HARDWARE

6: A review of software for geographers *Diana Freeman*	16
7: CD-ROM technology in geography: potential and issues *Helen Warner*	18
8: Something old, something new, something borrowed – and something 'off the Internet' *David Hassell*	20
9: Geographers on the Internet *Chris Durbin and Roger Sanders*	22
10: Making the most of images *David Hassell and ITWG*	27
11: Presentation software *Steve Rogers*	30
12: Whole-class computer activities *David Hassell*	32
13: Satellite images and IT capability *Michael Barnett and Mike Milton*	34
14: A guide to geographical information systems *Diana Freeman, David Green and David Hassell*	36
15: Visualisation software: a new aid to learning *David Holmes*	38

ICT TRAINING

16: Developing novice teacher ICT competence *Liz Newcombe*	41
17: Will you get some training? *David Hassell*	46

RESOURCES

Sources and websites	48

Introduction

A regular feature of *Teaching Geography* is the 'Information and Communications Technology' (ICT) section - usually one article in each issue. Over the years, these have built up into a collection of relevant, practical and useful articles which inform teachers about resources that are available and show how other geography teachers are using ICT.

High-tech geography: ICT in secondary schools brings together articles that appeared during the period 1994 to 1999. There is a temptation to assume, with ICT, that anything written about it on Tuesday is out of date on Wednesday. What we found, however, when we looked at some of the older articles, was that minor details apart, they have stood the test of time well, so they are included. For the most part, they appear here in their original form except that as far as possible, prices and website addresses have been updated.

A companion volume *High-tech geography: ICT in primary schools* brings together articles from *Primary Geographer*. Together these two publications provide a rich source of advice and information across the primary/secondary phases, demonstrating how progression with ICT through the key stages can be achieved.

The articles in this publication fall into three broadly defined sections:

- The articles in the first section are curriculum related. They describe where and how ICT can be built into schemes of work and how assessment and progression issues can be addressed. Specific applications of ICT to coursework and to GNVQ courses are also addressed.

- Articles in the second section review hardware and software and illustrate how these can be applied to geography teaching and learning. Although information on some of the products dates rapidly, the articles are often valid for several years after publication.

- Articles in the third section relate ICT training to novice and to experienced teachers respectively. Since the government is determined to raise the level of ICT capability in the teaching workforce, and therefore the capability of the students they teach, few geography teachers will remain untouched by the new proposals.

ICT or IT?

The difference in the terms 'information and communications technology' (ICT) and 'information technology' (IT) is often confusing. Pickford and Hassell define ICT and IT thus:

- 'Information and communications technology' refers to the computing and communications that support teaching and learning, where the focus is on the curriculum subject being taught, not on the technology skills. ICT is not just about computers: it also covers the use of fax machines, tape recorders and cameras.

- 'IT' refers to the students' knowledge and understanding of the technology and their ability to apply it, as stated in the IT National Curriculum. Here the focus is on the technology skills. (Pickford and Hassell, 1999, p. 3).

Sheila King
December 1999

Reference
Pickford, T. and Hassell, D. (1999) *Planning for ICT and geography at key stages 1 and 2.* Sheffield/Coventry: GA/BECTa

Sheila King is Lecturer in Education at the Institute of Education, University of London, E-mail: s.king@ioc.ac.uk

ICT in the curriculum

1 Integrating ICT into schemes of work

David Gardner describes ICT developments within the geography curriculum at Raincliffe School (1991-97)

The integration of information technology into geography schemes of work at Raincliffe School began in 1991. A revision of the school's ICT policy led to the dismantling of the school computer room and the redistribution of existing computers into subject classrooms, together with the purchase of new computers for geography and history. Successive geography department development plans have led to the gradual integration of ICT into all geography schemes of work in key stage 3, together with the expansion of both hardware and software provision. Funding for this has been achieved in a variety of ways including the use of department capitation allowance and by approaching local businesses, such as Marks & Spencer.

There are currently two geography classrooms at Raincliffe School and each has four computers, three of which are multimedia, all stand-alone and linked to a printer. The latest development project in the geography department has been the conversion of an open space (which adjoins the two classrooms) into a computer room. This provides shared access to a further 13 Amstrads - donated to the school by a neighbouring further education college. These machines allow students to word-process text and produce spreadsheets and databases. The department also has its own data-logging weather station purchased by the Raincliffe School Association. The geography department has been actively involved in whole-school ICT developments, and has taken on whole-school responsibility for the introduction and development of several key areas of the IT programmes of study.

ICT has been integrated into geography schemes of work at two levels: activities which focus on whole year group ICT-led geography tasks, and IT activities for individual students or small groups as part of the geography lesson. The ultimate aim is that the computers will be used by some or all students in every lesson, as a tool to study geography. Figure 1 illustrates where ICT is currently integrated into the key stage 3 programme of study and gives examples of ICT activities.

Year 7 using an electronic atlas

This activity has been developed, in part, to introduce the use of an electronic atlas and for showing students how to locate places around the world. Only two computers in the classroom have the capability to run the *World Atlas* CD-ROM. The use of the electronic atlas is one of a number of tasks arranged in a circus of activities round which the students move during several lessons. The activities involve locating places around the world using an atlas, globe, satellite images, three *Geosafari* computer location games, as well as *World Atlas*. The skills introduced in this activity need to be consolidated, and opportunities provided for progression towards independent student use. In year 8, for example, students use the computer atlas to measure indicators of development. In year 9 independent research is encouraged as part of studies on Japan and France.

Year 8 local environmental issue

In year 8, ICT opportunities are integrated into the production of a class debate about sewage outfall at Scarborough at a mock public meeting. The class is divided into four groups, each of which represents a different group of people in Scarborough. Each group is issued with an assignment sheet outlining the tasks and each student in the group takes responsibility for one aspect of the work. The research tasks include searches of CD-ROMs such as *Encarta*, as well as newspapers. Each group produces a desktop-published flyer outlining their point of view. A questionnaire is word-processed and issued to a whole year group within school. Students in the group process the results and produce spreadsheets and charts. Some of the charts are pasted into the flyer. As the use of a video camera is also utilising ICT, students use this to interview staff, particularly the headteacher, about the issue. A final meeting of the group establishes a running order to the presentations. As part of the multimedia presentation by each group:

- charts are printed onto overhead transparencies;
- flyers are distributed to the audience;
- the video-taped interviews are shown; and
- computer-generated banners are displayed.

To give the proceedings added realism, a guest is invited to attend the meeting, either a representative from a local environmental group (for example) or the headteacher.

Year 9 weather reporting

As part of a unit of work on weather and climate, each class is given responsibility for running the department's data-logging weather station for a month. The class work together to create the spreadsheet, and establish a rota for individual students to enter the data for each day of the month. Students are encouraged to collect weather-related articles from local newspapers, e.g. on severe storms, flooding, cold temperatures, and they also obtain the latest weather satellite images from the Meteorological Office using the Internet. At the end of the month, the class work in groups to produce a chart for each element of the weather recorded. Students are given a complete set of charts, and satellite images. Additional information is provided such as weather charts from national newspapers (collected during the month) and video clips of televised weather forecasts. The students' task is to analyse all the information to: (a) identify weather patterns occurring during the month, and (b) establish the type of weather systems which passed over the area. This analysis takes the form of a report of approximately 250 words. After some teacher guidance through the data, the students draft the report for homework. In the next lesson each student word-processes their report and inserts a chart from the spreadsheet. The completed reports, together with newspaper articles and satellite images, are displayed

Year	Term	Topic	IT opportunity
7	autumn	Geographical skills	CD-ROM *World Atlas* - an activity to introduce the CD-ROM to all year 7 students. CD-ROM *Discover York* - activities on four and six figure grid references, and use of aerial photographs integrated into class activities
	autumn	Drainage basins	CD-ROM *Physical World* introductory task on how to research data off CD-ROM into word-processing package
	spring	Settlement and Burniston fieldwork	CD-ROM *Discover York* for land use areas. Introduce spreadsheets for all students from traffic survey conducted on fieldwork day, chart results, word-process enquiry
	summer	Weathering and erosion; rivers, coasts, Flamborough Head	CD-ROM *Physical World* - research topics and export to word-processing package
8	autumn	Economic activities Thorn Park Farm fieldwork	Word-process enquiry, make spreadsheet and chart land use data
	autumn	Plate tectonics	Case study for IT task either Mount St Helens volcanic eruption on San Francisco earthquake (1989) using Internet and CD-ROMs *Physical World, Encarta, Geodome, Violent Earth* for research. Students work in groups to produce desk-top published newspaper front page
	autumn	Population	Use of CD-ROM *World Atlas* to research population data for selected countries students to create charts of results for analysis
	spring	Development	Research task using CD-ROM *World Atlas* to investigate indicators of development
	spring	India	Research basic data about India using Internet; CD-ROMs *World Atlas, Encarta, Global Explorer* and desk-top publishing package. Group investigation using CD-ROM *Discover India* and other resources
	summer	Environmental concerns, sewage outfall fieldwork	Investigate aims of environmental groups using Internet. Class debate about local issue - conduct questionnaire in school, make spreadsheet and chart results; incorporate into desk-top published flyer for debate
	summer	North York Moors National Park	Make spreadsheet and chart data from National Park surveys, incorporate into word-processed analysis
9	autumn	Weather and climate	Data-logging, spreadsheets, word-processed weather report. Internet, MetFAX, CD-ROMs *Physical World* and *Windows on Weather*
	autumn	Ecosystems and rainforests	Research using Internet, CD-ROMs *World Atlas, Physical World, Encarta*; SATCOM Forest Module; desk-top publish news report
	autumn	Environmental hazards	Research Using Internet, CD-ROMs *World Atlas, Physical World, Encarta*
	spring	Shopping issues fieldwork	Creation of database of shopping questionnaire results by all students. Spreadsheets and charting of results incorporated into word-processed enquiry
	spring	France	Research using Internet, CD-ROMs *World Atlas, Encarta, Global Explorer*, charting of data to create desk-top published report
	summer	Japan	Research using Internet, CD-ROMs *World Atlas, Encarta, Global explorer*, charting of data to create desk-top published report
	summer	World trade	CD-ROM *World Atlas*

Figure 1: ICT opportunities in key stage 3 PoS.

around the school. Once the routine is established, students collect the data and produce the reports every month. In the first year of this activity the local newspaper published a whole page of these weather reports and charts and included photographs of each student next to their reports.

The tasks are differentiated in a variety of ways:

- by varying the number of weather elements to be recorded;
- by asking students to enter data into a previously prepared spreadsheet;
- by reducing the number of additional resources;
- by increasing the amount of teacher guidance in analysing the data in order to write the report.

This activity is an important component of the whole-school ICT portfolio of work.

References

GA/NCET (now BECTa) (1994) *Geography and IT: Shopping and traffic.* Sheffield/Coventry: GA/NCET.

The following resources are listed as used in Figure 1: *Discover York*, Ordnance Survey; *Discover India*, ActionAid; *Encarta '96 World Atlas*, Microsoft; *Geosafari* game – available from good toy shops; *Global Explorer*, Koch Media; *METFAX*, Meteorological Office; *The Physical World*, Nelson Multimedia/YITM; *Windows on Weather*, AU Enterprises Ltd; *SATCOM Forest Module*, WWF; *Violent Earth*, Wayland Multimedia; *World Atlas*, various sources, including Koch Media.

The approach used at Raincliffe School not only enhances the quality of enjoyment of geography, but also reinforces geography's position in the whole-school curriculum. ■

David Gardner is Head of Humanities at Raincliffe School, Scarborough, North Yorkshire.

ICT in the curriculum

2 Planning for progression in IT activities

Photo: Richard Greenhill.

Helen Warner discusses the planning of progression in Information Technology and geography (1997)

In July 1997, secondary school teachers will be required to assign each year 9 student with a level for their attainment in the national curriculum foundation subjects, this includes information technology. In recent reports the Office for Standards in Education (OFSTED) has given much attention to IT, for example:

'There is evidence of much routine practice of low-level skills [at key stage 3]' (OFSTED, 1995).

So what is progression in IT? In *Approaches to IT Capability - key stage 3*, published by the National Council for Educational Technology (now BECTa), it is suggested that progression in IT arises:

'where students acquire new skills as a response to the needs of an activity. The consolidation of these skills, in a range of contexts, together with discussion and reflection on their effectiveness, leads to IT capability' (NCET, 1995).

Geography departments can provide a key role in enabling students to consolidate their IT capability by utilising data handling, word-processing and mapping packages within their studies. These ICT tools should help students to research, express opinions and present information about a particular issue such as deforestation. Students should also be encouraged to look for spatial patterns, investigate relationships and 'test' hypotheses on themes, e.g. weather and development. So, how can you ensure progression?

Planning for progression

Long-term key stage planning will ensure that your students receive regular experience of using ICT in the classroom. Such planning must take progression into account so that all of your students become familiar with a software package, operate it effectively and decide when to use it. This means planning ICT experiences for students within each year at key stage 3. Figure 1 gives an example of some data handling activities included in a planning matrix from year 7 to year 9.

In addition, planning for progression is closely linked to planning for assessment. Everyone would agree that it is a waste of students' time to be engaged in work that is either too easy or too hard. Similarly, expectations for year 7 will not be the same as year 10. Therefore, having decided the 'topic' for a period, your medium- and short-term plan also needs to address progression.

A model for planning progression into a unit of work

For any unit or scheme of work, a description of attainment, at a range of levels, is necessary. I propose that teachers use two or three tiers. This would depend on the age of the students and the nature of the activity. Bear in mind that some activities are more limiting in their scope for assigning attainments to than others. Your descriptions can then be used to assess a student's attainment at the end of a unit of work, and, rather like the end-of-key stage level descriptions, can provide a 'best fit' description of what the student knows, understands and

Figure 1: An example of data handling activities within a key stage 3 planning matrix.

Year	Autumn	Spring	Summer
7	Local area and other places (includes climate settlement and economic): comparisons database – 'find the place'	Environmental issues: rainforest/ Antarctica – CD-ROM research, Internet	Settlement: shopping survey database Population: population pyramids;
8	Weather and Climate: weather database investigation Ecosystems – CD-ROM	Tectonic processes: CD-ROM research, Internet	Population changes; Italy spreadsheet exercise Population and resources: India exercise
9	Geomorphological processes: river fieldwork, spreadsheet cross-sections and flood hydrographs	Development: Global database/mapping (geographical information systems)	Economic activities: spreadsheet comparisons Settlement: local conflict issue - database/GIS

DIFFERENCES IN DEVELOPMENT – Year 9

Minimum attainment Level 3/4	Intermediate attainment Level 5/6	Higher attainment Level 7/8
Students can access the stored information in a database file, sort countries and group them according to prescribed characteristics such as urban population, infant mortality. Students follow straightforward lines of enquiry but understand the need to frame questions carefully. This is supported by teacher-produced sheet(s) which help students with what to do. They know that data is only reliable if it is collected and entered accurately. Those that use a mapping package, work as part of a group, using a crib sheet. They select one or two statistics to map and answer questions about the global patterns found, largely using teacher-set questions.	These students are working more autonomously. They may start with a hypothesis suggested by the teacher, such as 'Wealth means health'. After some initial help, students work out what searches or sorts are required. Some students may, with help, suggest an appropriate further hypothesis of their own which they then 'test'. After initial guidance, some students start to interpret scatter graphs; look at relationships between measurable data sets, e.g. GNP and infant mortality, and annotate print-outs to indicate what is being shown. In discussion, it is apparent that students at this level understand some possible problems with average country-based statistics and may relate this to their own previous survey experience. Those students that use a mapping package are able to make some simple predictions about the spatial pattern they expect to see (before mapping it). They can interpret patterns as displayed and present conclusions that are consistent with the evidence.	These students can work largely autonomously. They are able to work with both teacher-set and their own hypotheses. They are able to interpret and use scatter graphs, where appropriate, and after initial help may generate and explain correlation values. They can decide whether to use a database or spreadsheet as necessary. These students are able to communicate possible problems with using data, proving that they understand the complexity of factors which may affect the quality of life in a specific country. They may do some research, e.g. from a database available on the Internet, to find additional information for their own investigation. Those students that use a mapping package can do so confidently. For instance, they can discuss the way that changing the intervals can affect the resultant spatial display, thus highlighting the limitations of working with automatically-produced maps. These students may choose to link their own data to a map for a project.

Figure 2: Example of progression within a year 9 activity.

can do. This means that work can be planned which will enable students to achieve within the range. It also avoids trying to work out what IT the students might achieve after planning and activity. Where there is no clear indication of the possible progression within activities, there is often a 'ceiling' of standards of achievement which individual students can attain. In some cases this means that some students are working below their capability. It is important to bear in mind that activities which do not address higher-level as well as lower-level attainment (particularly in year 9) will make progress across the key stage limited.

Figure 2 shows an example of year 9 students' progression within an activity. Here, the minimum attainment is for the least able/experienced. The intermediate tier is for the majority of students and the higher tier for the most able/experienced.

The purpose of a summary statement is to give a feel for where the learning intentions are pitched. The intention is not to teach to level descriptions, but to suggest what attainment might look like at this level. Much ICT work in schools comes from the students' work within other subject areas; therefore, this approach may make it easier for teachers to record attainment and plan for progression.

The example shown in Figure 2 is based on an activity in *Investigating Aspects of Human Geography* (GA/NCET, 1996). Undertaking such an activity raises a number of key questions including:

- What prior database or spreadsheet work have students done in this school?
- Will we be able to cover the higher level work in geography?
- What in-service training needs do we have?
- How many computers would be needed for this activity?
- How do we get access to the computers?
- What support sheets will we need to prepare and what already exists?
- How will we organise students to ensure all are challenged?
- How can we collaborate with the IT co-ordinator? (IT work in geography needs to be part of the whole-school planning framework for IT and, therefore, collaboration with your IT co-ordinator will be crucial.)

Reference

NCET (1995) *Approaches to IT Capability – key stage 3*. Coventry: NCET.
OFSTED (1995) *Information Technology – A review of inspection findings 1993/94*. London: HMSO.
The following Geography and IT Support Project publications are available from the Geographical Association or BECTa (while stocks last):
Shopping and Traffic Fieldwork (1994) £15.00;
Investigating Weather Data (1994) £22.50;
Investigating Aspects of Human Geography (1996) £22.50;
Using IT to Enhance Geography – case studies at key stages 3 and 4 (1995) £7.50.

Helen Warner is ICT adviser for the London Borough of Tower Hamlets.

ICT in the curriculum

3 Assessing IT in geography

The activities shown in Figure 1 were designed to contribute to a range of IT and Geography National Curriculum Levels, depending on the individual students' ability, as outlined below:

IT Levels
2 Students use IT-based models or simulations to investigate options.
3 Students use IT-based models or simulations to help them make decisions.
4 Students use IT-based models or simulations to explore patterns or

Keith Whiddon illustrates how activities in geography can contribute to the assessment of IT capabilities (1998)

There is a role for geographers to support the assessment of students' IT capability no matter how your school organises the delivery of ICT, either across the curriculum or through IT lessons. With a specific IT requirement and the range of opportunities for using ICT in geography many departments often support the delivery of ICT. This might include taking on the development of skills through teaching spreadsheets or databases or by applying the skills students have developed in other lessons.

The assessment of IT capability relies on a teacher's professional judgement of the level which best describes a student's work. It is therefore important that assessment is made by the teacher who is teaching the lesson. It is unrealistic to expect IT co-ordinators to make a secure assessment based solely on the print-outs from a lesson they have not seen.

A number of geography teachers in Surrey delivered and assessed IT in year 7 by using a spreadsheet version of *The Anglo-Saxon Settlement Game*. This well-known exercise is used to teach concepts relating to settlement and least-cost location. The game also provides a simple, but effective introduction to the benefits of computer modelling. Using a computer for this exercise adds value over conventional teaching methods in that it does the long-winded and rather mechanical calculations. This leaves more time for the students to explore the concepts involved. Computer modelling involves the ability to:

- establish sets of rules based on hypotheses;
- test these rules by entering data;
- alter the data to ask 'what if' questions and analyse the effects of changing the rules.

The Anglo-Saxon Settlement Game

Your tribe has discovered an uninhabited river valley in which to make a permanent settlement. All the things needed to make your settlement a success can be found here, but unfortunately not all at the same location. Scouts have recommended three possible sites (A, B and C). As no one site is ideal, some sort of compromise must be found.

The tribe's elders have identified five main requirements of your settlement (in no particular order of importance):

- a place that is easy to defend
- fresh water
- grazing land
- a ready supply of timber
- arable land

Q1. Say why each of the above is important and suggest where each might be found.

Clearly some of these things are required on a daily basis, while others are needed less often.

Q2. In groups, award a weighting, on a scale of 0 to 9, to each of the above requirements. For example, if you consider that nearness to grazing land is the most important factor, award it 9. If you consider nearness to fresh water to be of limited importance, award it a low number. Write down the reasons for your choices. Enter this data into the spreadsheet.

To be a really successful settlement, you need to be as near as possible to the things you need the most, otherwise the people will waste a lot of time and energy moving around and carrying things.

Q3. Measure the approximate distance (to the nearest 50m) from each of the possible sites to the nearest location of timber, water, defence, grazing and arable land. Enter this data into the spreadsheet.

When you have entered all of this data into the spreadsheet, the computer will calculate which of the sites is best for your needs.

Q4. Such a site is said to have the least cost. Explain what this means.

With time, circumstances may change. For example, if the threat of attack was no longer an issue then the need to be near to a defensive location would not be so important. Developments in technology could mean that it becomes possible to cut and carry larger quantities of wood at the same time, thus reducing the need to be so near to a supply of timber.

Q5. In your groups, discuss these and other possible changes. Look at the map. Predict what effect such changes might have on which settlement has the least-cost. Say why this may happen.

Q6. Using the spreadsheet, explore the effects of such changes by altering the weightings. Describe and explain your results. Did the least-cost location change? If so, which factor caused this change?

Q7. Why do you think a spreadsheet was used to assist with this activity? How would you have done the tasks without one?

Q8. Imagine that you have to explain what a spreadsheet is to a person who has never used one before. Think about the different ways in which you have used the spreadsheet to help with this activity.

Figure 1: The Anglo-Saxon Settlement Game – students' sheet.

relationships and make simple predictions about the consequence of their decision-making.
5 Students explore the effects of changing the variables in a computer model.

Geography Levels
2 Students select information from resources provided. They use this information and their own observations to ask and respond to questions about places.
3 Students offer reasons for some of their observations and judgements about places.
4 Students begin to describe geographical patterns and appreciate the importance of location in understanding places.
5 Students describe and begin to offer explanations for geographical patterns.

(DFE, 1995a, b)

IT capability is not simply concerned with IT skills such as 'using a spreadsheet'. There is also a need to develop knowledge and understanding. In a recent report Gabriel Goldstein states that:

'many lessons tend to develop low-level skills at the expense of knowledge and understanding. Few encourage the gradual development and improvement of interesting and substantial pieces of work in IT over a period, which enhance knowledge, understanding and critical judgement in using IT' (Goldstein, 1997, p. 15).

The questions in Figure 1 are designed to assess the skills, knowledge and understanding of the modelling aspect of the IT National Curriculum. During the lessons teachers observed, facilitated and supported their students as necessary. During observation the opportunity was taken to identify the contribution made by individual students within groups and this was supplemented by questioning. Teachers found it helpful to make brief notes in order to record useful assessment evidence.

If successfully completed by students, questions 1 to 4 of the activity in Figure 1 would contribute to National Curriculum IT Level 3. This requires that 'students use IT-based models or simulations to help them make decisions'.

Question 5 tests the students' understanding of the concepts of least-cost location and how the spreadsheet model works by asking the student to make predictions of 'What would happen if ...?'. The ability to make predictions based on secure understanding of the concepts involved contributes to Level 4. This requires that 'students use ICT-based models or simulations to explore patterns or relationships and

Photo: **Sally Greenhill.**

make simple predictions about the consequence of their decision making'.

Question 6 is related to Question 5, but here the student must also alter the variables of the model. If this is done purposefully, in a way that clearly demonstrates understanding, it contributes to Level 5. This requires that 'students explore the effects of changing the variables in a computer model'

Questions 7 and 8, which focus upon students describing, explaining and reflecting upon their work, were found to be particularly appropriate homework tasks, given that no access to a computer is required. A vital part of IT capability is to demonstrate a reflective aspect and these types of questions also test understanding.

Conclusion
This assessment was, therefore, based on a combination of:

- written work;
- computer print-outs annotated by the students;
- homework exercises to test knowledge and understanding; and
- teacher observation and questioning to determine the individual student's contribution to the activity.

This article provides a starting point for a discussion on the assessment of both IT and geography. ■

Author's note
If you have been involved in delivering elements of the IT curriculum and would be willing to share your experiences, Dave Hassell would like to hear from you. Assessment is one of the areas in which the GA's IT Working Group hopes to build up a number of examples of good practice to disseminate either through the pages of *Teaching Geography* or as a short booklet.

References
DFE (1995a) *IT in the National Curriculum.* London: HMSO.
DFE (1995b) *Geography in the National Curriculum.* London: HMSO.
Goldstein, G. (1997) *Information Technology in English Schools – A commentary on inspection findings 1995-6.* London: HMI.

Keith Whiddon is a County Consultant/Inspector for IT in the Surrey Education Service, an ex-geography teacher and is a member of the GA's IT Working Group.

ICT in the curriculum

4 Using ICT in coursework

David Hassell outlines the opportunities and provides some examples (1996)

The Geography IT Support Project leaflet *Geography – A Student's Entitlement for IT* which was distributed free to all maintained secondary schools in 1994, outlined the benefits that ICT could provide and suggested that students studying geography are entitled to use ICT to:

- enhance their geographical enquiry skills;
- gain access to a wide range of geographical knowledge and information sources;
- deepen their understanding of environmental and spatial relationships;
- experience alternative images of people, place and environment;
- consider the wider impact of IT on people, place and environment.

These statements have become well accepted as fundamental tenets and have been built into the key stage 3 geography guidance produced by SCAA (now QCA) and NCET (now BECTa). They have also provided the basis for the materials produced by the geography IT Support Project and a range of other work in schools.

ICT can be used in all areas of the geography curriculum. However, it is often stated that with limited hardware resources it is best to employ ICT where it can most enhance the learning experience. Coursework provides an ideal place to enable students to use the IT skills they will be building through their school career to improve their geography work.

Probably the most obvious benefit is that of liberating students from tedious and repetitive mechanical tasks, enabling them to spend longer on the geographical evaluation of the material they are working with.

The *GCSE Criteria for Geography* (SCAA, 1995) make a positive statement about the use of ICT by stating that all syllabuses should give students opportunities to:

'... acquire and apply the skills and techniques – including those of mapwork, fieldwork and IT – needed to conduct geographical enquiry.'

The document goes on to assert that syllabuses must require:

'... the development of geographical enquiry skills (including, where appropriate, the use of IT).'

It is unlikely that a stronger statement will appear in the near future because of the implications that this might have for the resourcing of examination teaching.

In some examination syllabuses, the use of ICT in coursework is becoming more commonplace. For example, the NEAB Geography Syllabus C 'welcomes the use of IT'. The course booklet does highlight the need to ensure that work is the student's own, that any primary data must be available for scrutiny, and that the use of ICT must be declared. Students are usually able to provide coursework in a word-processed format which contains graphs, charts and maps which have been produced using a computer. A thorny issue in the past has been that the use of ICT can hide whether students actually know how to produce the

Software/hardware	One potential application
Word-processing	In any enquiry to support students' intended writing, where they can draft and redraft reports.
Drawing, painting and desktop-publishing packages	Tools for illustration in any type of material, e.g. combining text and images to provide a high-quality method for designing survey sheets.
Spreadsheets	To provide a tool for evaluating and modelling a range of decisions, e.g. evaluating routes in an enquiry on the location of a new bypass. Using a weighting scheme the spreadsheet provides opportunities to evaluate many different options effectively.
Databases	To provide access to data, explore patterns and relationships and display results effectively. For instance, in an enquiry on tourism a database of questionnaire results would enable the students to explore links between gender, age and holiday location.
CD-ROM	To provide access to a wide range of information and deepen understanding of spatial relationships, e.g. a census CD-ROM can support an enquiry into the contention that quality of life can be low in urban and rural areas.
Mapping and geographical information systems (GIS) software	To explore spatial relationships by querying a database and displaying the results spatially. For instance, a GIS can support investigations into the link between the economic and social factors and regional inequalities in India.
Portables in the field	Using portables in the field enables direct entry of information from a questionnaire or observations. This enables initial analysis to determine whether further measurements or questionnaires need to be carried out, e.g. checking that mistakes have not been made in the collection of river data.
Data logging	To record data accurately over a period, which could not be achieved manually, e.g. to explore the link between local facility use and daily weather. Data from automatic weather stations can be exported to a spreadsheet or database for comparison and analysis.
Remote sensing	To provide access to richer images of an area which can illustrate change over time and be manipulated. For instance, imagery of the local area can be used to support an enquiry into the actual and potential loss of urban green space.
Internet	The Internet can provide access to a wealth of resources. For example, people's views and information on issues related to the Kobe earthquake can be obtained when investigating the impact of physical processes.

Table 1: **Opportunities for using ICT to support coursework.**

graph or map, etc. Most examining groups seem happy with an approach where the students should produce one graph by hand to illustrate that they do have the knowledge and skills to complete the task and the rest can be produced using a computer. It should be remembered that the choice of chart or map representation is in itself a geographical skill and that the indiscriminate production of the computer-generated material should be discouraged.

Benefits of ICT

Information skills are central to geographical enquiry. Students are expected to consider what information they need; research a topic effectively; carry out an investigation, often using large quantities of data (possibly as a collaboratively collected resource); analyse and synthesise the data; evaluate and draw conclusions. Students should be developing information-handling skills in IT throughout key stages 3 and 4. The application of these skills in geography can assist students with the development and completion of better coursework.

Coursework often involves statistical evaluation, the production of a large number of maps and graphs, or the sorting and evaluation of a large amount of information. The use of ICT can release students from mechanistic chores and provide more quality time for the evaluation and interpretation of the materials they have gathered or are investigating. All too frequently, coursework is criticised for producing a great deal of information with little critical comment from the students. Using ICT in this way can also provide special needs students with the confidence to move beyond simple collection and display.

Too often the word-processed report is simply a way of producing a neat version of work. Where students are encouraged to use the word-processor from the start, there is evidence that their extended writing can be improved. Students can be provided with outline structures which are supportive and the process of planning, drafting and redrafting can improve report quality. This is particularly true for those with poorer writing skills or with special educational needs.

The continuing development of the range of CD-ROMs and on-line services, such as the Internet, provides access to new sources of geographical information, mainly secondary evidence and alternative images of people, places and environments. There is an enormous range of resources, from statistics and general information to weather satellite imagery and other primary data from many sites around the globe. As with any other resource, students will need help to use them effectively. However, these resources provide enhanced opportunities for supporting students' own research and enquiries.

A number of ICT devices provide the opportunity to gather primary data quickly and efficiently. There are automatic weather stations, weather satellite receivers and data-logging equipment which can record stream flow, temperature and other environmental factors. Some developers have identified that the data-logging devices produced for the science curriculum could be adapted to become useful tools for geographers and some have plans to produce devices specifically for the subject.

Information and communications technology provides a wide range of opportunities, from being able to type up the text to the use of geographical information systems and automatic data collection in the field. Table 1 provides some examples of such opportunities.

Issues associated with ICT

Despite the advantages, there is a major issue in most schools about the provision of access for all. At the moment it is unlikely that a school could provide a whole year with enough access to ICT, so that they are able take advantage of all possible benefits. However, it is possible to stagger assessed modules across the year, and although there is no perfect answer, the following strategies may be helpful. ICT priority access could be arranged for those students who:

- have enquiries that are very demanding of processing, e.g. large databases;
- need access to large data sources, e.g. CD-ROM or the Internet;
- need most support to produce extended writing;
- do not have access in other lessons or at home.

There may be opportunities to work with the IT co-ordinator to investigate how greater access can be obtained, by considering how the coursework completed by students might contribute to the core IT skills that are being delivered.

Some schools have identified a link with the home which can help with access. The proportion of homes with a computer is increasing dramatically and it is possible to use this resource. Whilst it is possible simply to suggest that students use the computers at home, it might be more profitable to provide some guidance for students (and their parents) about what is expected from the use of ICT to support their enquiry. This can ensure that students do not waste large amounts of time. (If this approach is investigated, the issue of the transfer of viruses should be addressed.)

There has always been an issue about whether the work that students complete at home is their own, and the use of home computers may add to this problem. However, discussion with students can soon identify those with real understanding. Teachers have to be aware of

Skills should include the use of IT.   Photo: Sally and Richard Greenhill.

this and employ strategies to encourage students to complete tasks correctly.

Another issue of which teachers and students have to be aware is the apparent authority of computer-generated materials or information. Where students are looking for information from a CD-ROM or the Internet, it is often assumed that what they find and present must be true, because a computer has provided it. Like all other forms of information, this has been selected and edited by a person and therefore may well be only one view of the facts. There is also the issue of assuming that the first result will be correct, be it the first type of graph selected or the search of a database. Students must beware of this and should be encouraged to question outcomes, e.g. is this the right type of chart for the data plotted, or was the query addressed to the database the appropriate one to obtain the desired result?

Case studies

Marriotts School, Stevenage

At Marriotts there has been a gradual increase in the use of ICT in assessed coursework. Work with ICT divides into two types: co-ordinated, class-based activities and individual assignments. Two of the class-based activities are a shopping survey and a role-play activity based on siting a holiday complex on a Caribbean island.

In the shopping survey the class carries out an annual survey of the shops in a nearby town, completing pedestrian flow counts and a number of other activities. The students then enter the shop premises information into a spreadsheet which can be used with a mapping program to display the occupancy and use of the shops and services. Each year this builds on previous surveys and allows the students to compare changes over time. The students then identify their own hypotheses which they will test. One example is to investigate the link between change, unoccupancy and position in the centre with relation to pedestrian flow.

The location exercise is a role-play which uses a CD-ROM as a support resource. The students investigate the development of a new holiday complex on St Lucia. They interrogate the information stored on the CD-ROM to investigate a number of possible locations, using an environmental assessment. The class then has a debate before each student decides whether the resort should be completed and, if so, where, writing a report to explain and justify his or her choice.

All the students have the opportunity to use ICT for their individual assignments and fieldwork should they so wish. Until recently the take-up has been quite low, although there is evidence that more students are beginning to use ICT to produce their ordinary

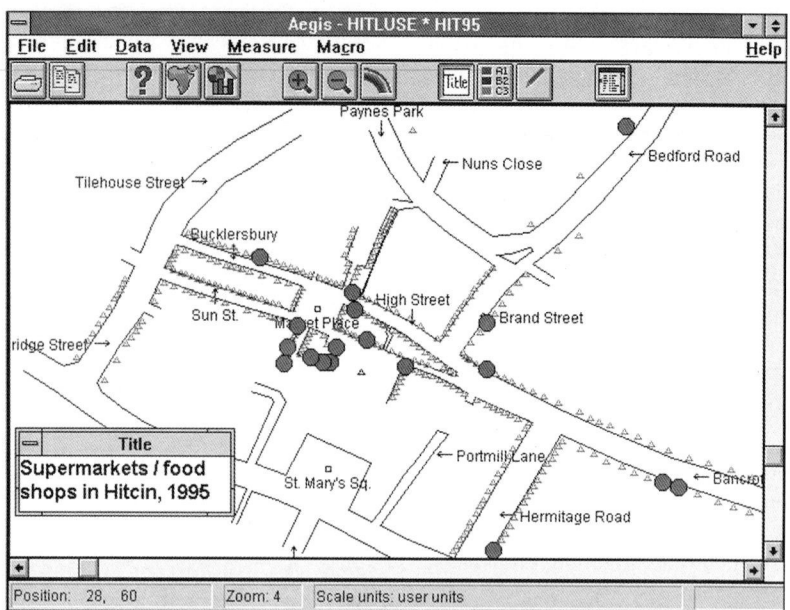

Figure 1: An example of the distribution maps produced by pupils.

assignments. This is the result of the school's ICT policy, which is ensuring that students obtain a continuous and progressive experience of ICT through the school.

The department is keen to develop the use of ICT in coursework. They have seen particular benefits in that students now spend longer on the investigation and the analysis of their work.

Bodmin Community College

The course taught at this college does not have individual student assignments but a series of assessed portfolio tasks, each of which provides 6 per cent of the final marks. The geography department is developing the portfolio activities so that each group of students has some ICT-based tasks during the course. Over the next year it is hoped to construct more enquiries where there is a range of possible activities supported by ICT.

One example is an investigation into urban structure. The unit starts with fieldwork in two areas of Plymouth, the CBD and a residential area. The students identify their hypotheses and then have the opportunity to use ICT to develop their data capture sheets which they will use in the field. When the students return from their fieldwork they can use spreadsheets, databases and word-processors to analyse and present their findings. As part of the follow-up work the students can use one of the census CD-ROMs to investigate differences between the two areas of the city. The next element of the unit is to investigate similar areas in a city in a less economically developed country, in this case Lima in Peru. The students can have access to the SATCOM software and two of the electronic atlases which they use as a resource for images, data and text to support the investigation and report writing which completes the task.

A second example is based on part of the physical systems module completed by year 10 students. In the section on weather and climate the department provides students with opportunities to use a range of ICT resources to support their investigations. The school has a weather satellite receiving station for obtaining up-to-date weather imagery. It also has a range of CD-ROMs with information on weather and climate, and this year students have started to obtain information from the Internet for use in their activities.

King Edward VI School, Lichfield

In the syllabus used in this department, the coursework component is wholly based on students conducting individual investigations. The department encourages the students to use ICT which should build on the IT taught at key stage 3. An increasing number of students are using ICT in their investigations, although there is considerable variety in the scope of the ICT use. Many students using ICT will word-process their work and others will use generic software in a variety of ways. Most investigations start with an initial exploration of a central theme by the whole group, from which each student will then develop an individual investigation.

The most commonly used pieces of software are a spreadsheet and a database. Two examples are work on environmental quality along a transect and an investigation of work patterns using a questionnaire to collect primary data.

In the environmental quality example, the students collaborate on the fieldwork. This involves an evaluation using a set of criteria scored on a positive and negative scale along a transect in the local area. Once back in school, the students enter the information into a spreadsheet, which

Figure 2: Analysis of environmental quality data by students at King Edwards VI School, Lichfield

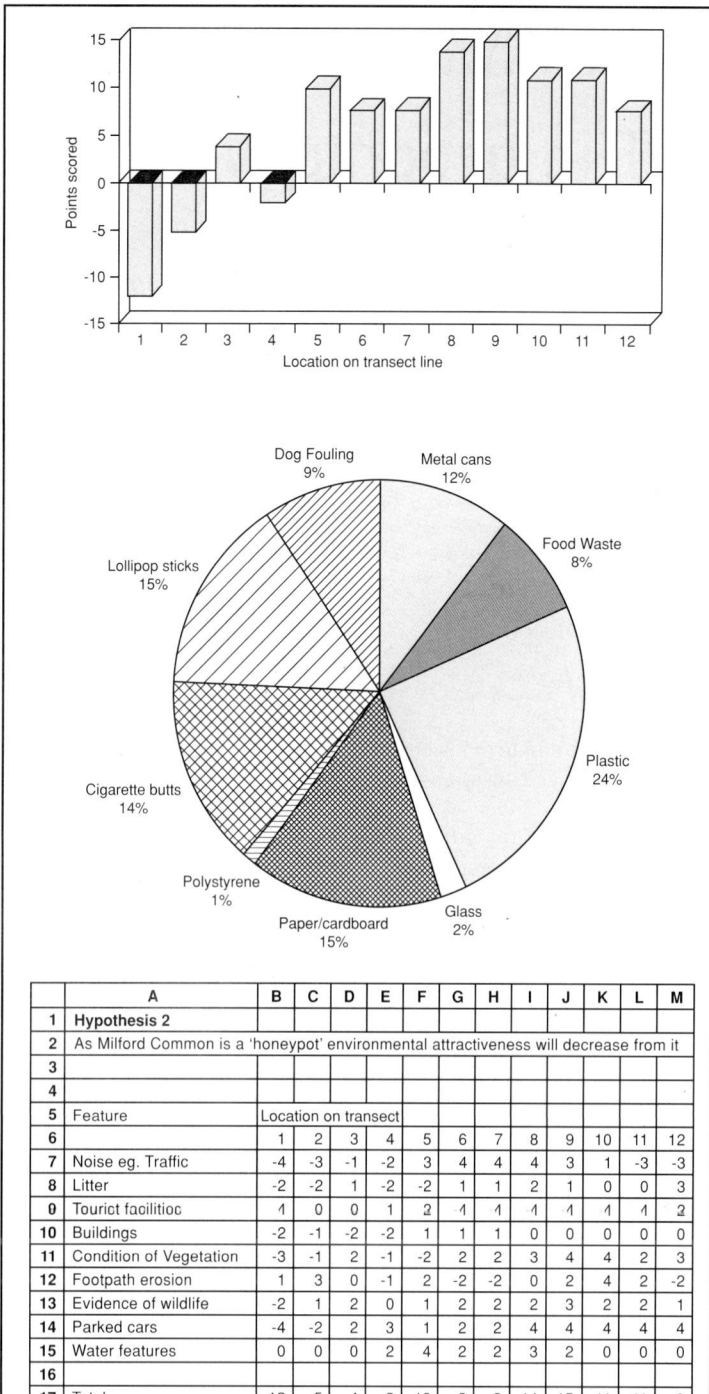

they can then use to analyse the results by calculating some straightforward statistics. The students complete one chart by hand, normally that of the totals, and then use the spreadsheet's charting facilities to chart and compare the data according to their own hypotheses (Figure 2).

In the second example, students conduct a questionnaire on the patterns of employment and the journeys to work. This information is entered into a database for analysis. Again, students are expected to develop their own questions to explore, for example, to compare the patterns associated with full and part-time employment in relation to the type of transport used and the distance travelled to work. From this the students can produce charts and print-outs of database queries to exemplify their work.

The teachers have felt that the use of ICT has been beneficial in a number of ways. Apart from motivating students, an interesting element has been that students have been willing to explore the different types of graph and chart that are available, in order to identify which is appropriate. The use of ICT has extended the written analysis of many students and enabled them to produce more charts. Most importantly, it was felt that the speed with which graphs could be produced and data analysed contributed to students spending more time exploring the geographical concepts on which the enquiry was focused.

Conclusion

There is a wide range of opportunities which ICT can bring to support coursework, despite the limitations of resources and time. These opportunities will increase as teacher experience, hardware, software and support materials develop. However, ICT can be a liberating influence and can provide opportunities for improving student achievements.

When developing the use of ICT for your GCSE coursework, the secondary entitlement leaflet is a good starting-point. This provides a practical checklist of activities and some suggestions about where to start. Another valuable place to gain some support and advice is a local school which might already be using ICT in this way. In addition, the Geography and IT Support Project materials and the IT feature in Teaching Geography will provide a range of ideas. One important task is to look at your examining group's statement on the use of ICT. Most follow the guidelines suggested in the introduction, but it is important to ensure that something you identify is acceptable to your examining group. ■

Editor's note:

Since this article was written, digital cameras have become increasingly affordable and are now a frequently-used resource in coursework (see also pages 27-29).

Acknowledgements

Many thanks to Maggie Hutchinson, Paul Tyrrell, Margaret Walker and Helen Warner for their time and contributions.

Further reading

Both of the following leaflets are available free from the GA or NCET (now BECTa).
GA/NCET (1994) *CD-ROMs for Geography*. Sheffield/Coventry: GA/NCET.
GA/NCET (1995) *Geography – A Student's Entitlement for IT*. Sheffield/Coventry: GA/NCET.
GA/NCET (1995-96) *Geography IT support materials: Shopping and Traffic Fieldwork*, £15.00. *Investigating Weather Data*, £22.50. *Investigating Aspects of Human Geography*, £22.50.
GA/NCET (1995) *Using IT to Enhance Geography – Case Studies at Key Stages 3 and 4*. Sheffield/Coventry: GA/NCET.
NCET (1994) *Approaches to IT Capability – key stage 3* (out of print). Coventry: NCET.
SCAA (1995) *GCSE Criteria for Geography*. London: HMSO.

David Hassell is Head of Curriculum and Institutional Development for Schools, British Educational Communications and Technology Agency (BECTa); e-mail: david_hassell@becta.org.uk

ICT in the curriculum

5 ICT in geography-related GNVQ

> **David Hassell** outlines some ways of supporting GNVQ Leisure & Tourism courses with ICT (1997)

An increasing number of schools and all further education colleges run GNVQ courses as an option for their students. Although there is evidence of geographers contributing to a wide range of GNVQs, it is in Leisure & Tourism courses that most geographers teach.

IT is an integral part of GNVQ courses as a key skill in which all students must become competent. However, in many institutions this element is taught as a separate aspect in its own timetabled slot and not as an integrated skill. In many courses, students may have considerable opportunity to develop their competence and confidence with ICT, sometimes using information related to the subject area. Rarely is ICT seen as a natural tool to support the wide spectrum of students' learning.

Many tutors supporting GNVQ courses may themselves be novices in the use of ICT. This article aims to provide an introduction to the potential of ICT and to illustrate some of the opportunities that can be found in institutions around the country.

What can ICT offer?

1993 saw the launch of a number of DfEE-funded projects to support the teaching and learning of subject areas through the use of ICT. The Geography and IT Support Project decided that it was vital to have a leaflet which introduced tutors to key ways ICT could enhance and support the teaching and learning of geography. The leaflet, *Geography – a student's entitlement to IT* (GA/NCET, 1994), was written for secondary schools, but the authors took great care to ensure that the guiding principles were appropriate across the age range taught in schools and colleges. These are that students studying geography are entitled to use ICT to:

- enhance their skills of geographical enquiry;
- gain access to a wide range of geographical knowledge and information sources;
- deepen their understanding of environmental and spatial relationships;
- experience alternative images of people, place and environment; and
- consider the wider impact of IT on people, place and environment.

All of these principles are equally applicable to a GNVQ Leisure & Tourism course.

The range of opportunities

A huge range of opportunities for ICT to enhance the teaching and learning of a course exists. Much generic software, such as word-processing packages, databases and spreadsheets, can enhance teaching and learning in a variety of ways. There has also been a huge increase in the potential for this area with the proliferation of CD-ROMs and the range and scope of information on the Internet. Four examples of ICT approaches are given below.

Developing transferable skills

One of the main elements of the IT core is the development of basic skills in word-processing and the use of databases and spreadsheets. This can be supported in the different subject-focused course units in a range of ways. One example is selling a tourist or leisure attraction to different audiences. Students were provided with a word-processed file comprising a general description of a specialist resort in Spain. They started by discussing which people might be attracted to the resort in the summer and winter, and the range of visitors coming in the summer. Students were given the task of rewriting the text to appeal to three different audiences. They were given a maximum number of words and were asked to present the text in the form of a brochure. Once students had completed the rewrite, they were asked to devise a catchy title and lay out the text for a brochure.

The task is simple and effective and, because the students were encouraged to develop the three samples in parallel, they had to consider the issues of language and composition in relation to the type of audience while concentrating on a leisure and tourism component. This approach can also support differentiation because the original text can be provided in a variety of forms to support the less able and to challenge the more able.

Gathering and analysing information

All students will have to complete some investigations which involve the gathering and analysis of a reasonable quantity of data, e.g. compiling and analysing a questionnaire on leisure pursuits, or creating a resource base of possible attractions. Here, a database is an invaluable tool, and in creating one, students will develop and apply core IT skills as well as supplementing their investigation. Although it takes time to enter data into a database, there are considerable benefits: students can handle larger sets of data, produce a wide range of graphs and charts, and look for patterns and relationships. All of this can be achieved more quickly on a computer, leaving more time for the students to think through the implications of what they have found and present a reasoned report.

Electronic information sources

CD-ROMs

The range of CD-ROMs which can be used in relation to the Leisure & Tourism GNVQ is increasing very quickly because developers see the 'edu-tainment' sector as one in which they can guarantee high volume sales. Good examples are CD-ROM atlases and encyclopaedias which provide considerable information and support for this type of course. Many institutions use them in a number of ways, for example:

- as sources for background information on climate, scenery and features of individual countries (virtually any title will be of value, e.g. *Encarta World Atlas, 3D-Atlas, Grolier, Hutchinson's*);
- for investigating heritage and other tourist sites of interest (e.g. titles such as *Global Explorer*, and encyclopaedias);

- for investigating itineraries, routes at a range of scales (most atlases have street maps of the major cities of the world) and whether it is possible to fly between different places (using titles such as *Global Explorer*);
- for developing information-handling skills.

Internet

As more institutions gain access to the Internet they are finding increasing options for leisure and tourism studies. One example is Henley College which integrates Internet investigations into a range of Leisure & Tourism units at Advanced level GNVQ.

The number of travel and tourism companies, councils and other organisations (museums, theatres and sports), and sites which provide travel information (airline, ferry and bus timetables) on the World Wide Web, continues to expand. These offer opportunities for activities in a broad range of areas, four examples of which are:

- investigating and comparing methods for crossing to the Continent, e.g. using P&O, Hoverspeed and Eurostar;
- researching information on a particular location, e.g. a town or a country;
- developing an itinerary for a journey in the UK using British Rail or National Express;
- gathering information on leisure pursuits by placing a questionnaire on your web pages (most Internet access providers offer their account holders a few pages on their website which a school can take advantage of, and many colleges now have their own websites).

Multimedia

A number of institutions have provided student with the opportunity to present their research findings using multimedia authoring tools. Most institutions have done this by linking the activity to their core skills courses and have found it a valuable way of integrating the content with the IT elements. In one case, for example, students investigating the provision of services and products presented their findings in multimedia form. This does not have to involve the use of expensive or complex professional packages. At Halton College, students of different abilities developed presentations to support their Leisure & Tourism courses in a variety of ways: one Advanced level GNVQ student produced a multimedia tour of the Granada Studios.

One of the main advantages of multimedia is that it can provide a flexible non-linear method of presenting a range of mixed media. Thus, for example, students might use a map of a chosen tourist or leisure attraction site as a core resource, and, by clicking on various elements of the map, access information in a variety of forms such as pictures, text and sounds. Their presentations can be compared with the sort of information provision being developed by many leisure and tourism sites.

Integrating IT into GNVQ

If you are interested in developing the use of IT to support your Leisure & Tourism GNVQ courses, you might like to start with some of the ideas shown here. It is important that IT is an integral element rather than something that is bolted on. Look at the planning page in the entitlement document (GA/NCET, 1994) or read the GA/NCET publication *GNVQ - Integrating IT* which provides an excellent overview of how IT can support GNVQ courses. For those in further education there are opportunities in the QUILT programme for staff development. For further information on this programme, see the panel below. ■

Interesting website addresses
(All sites must be prefixed with http://)
www.becta.org.uk

A place to start searching –
www.yahoo.co.uk

Henley College – www.henleycol.ac.uk

Crossing to the Continent
Hoverspeed - www.hoverspeed.co.uk
P&O - www.poef.com
Scandinavian Seaways - www.scansea.com
Eurostar - www.eurostar.com/eurostar/eurostar.html

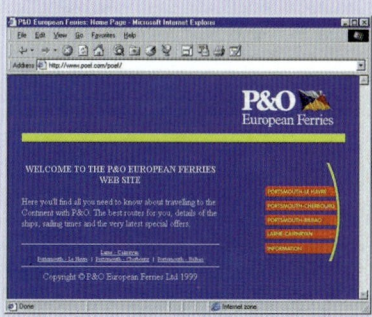

Leisure
Birmingham City Council - birmingham.gov.uk

Tourist Boards/virtual tours
ABTA - www.abtanet.com
The virtual tourist - www.vtourist.com
Rough Guides - roughguides.com
British Tourist Authority - www.bta.org.uk
Welsh Tourist Board - www.tourism.wales.gov.uk
SE England Tourist Board - www.seetb.org.uk
Manchester - www.u-net.com/manchester
New York - www.totalny.com
Brazil - www.brazil.org.uk

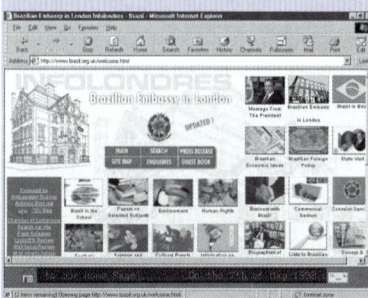

Travel
British Rail – www.railtrack.co.uk/travel
National Express – www.nationalexpress.co.uk

Acknowledgement
The author would like to thank Alan Marvel of New College, Swindon, for his comments and ideas.

References and further information
BECTa manages the Further Education Resources for Learning website which has a wide range of information and case studies on the use of information and communications technology in FE, including GNVQ: ferl.becta.org.uk

GA/NCET (1994) *Geography: A student's entitlement for IT*. Sheffield/Coventry: GA/NCET.

GA/NCET (1995) *CD-ROMs for Geography*, GA/NCET. Free copies of these two leaflets can be obtained by sending a first class A4 sae marked *Geography Entitlement* and/or *CD-ROMs* to the GA or NCET (now BECTa).

Marvell, A. and Smyth, T. (1995) 'Should you consider GCSE Travel & Tourism?', *Teaching Geography*, 21, 2, pp. 92-4.

NCET (1996) *GNVQ - Integrating IT*, Coventry: NCET (out of print).

> David Hassell is Head of Curriculum and Institutional Development for Schools, British Educational Communications and Technology Agency (BECTa); e-mail: david_hassell@becta.org.uk

Software and hardware

6 A review of software for geographers

Diana Freeman reports on a review of the software which is available for the geography teacher

Over the last year (1996-97) there has been much discussion about the quality and availability of educational software. National Council for Education and Technology (NCET, now BECTa), Schools Curriculum Association and Authority (SCAA, now QCA), and both the previous and current governments have identified the quality and availability of educational software as an important issue. In this light the Department for Education and Employment asked the eleven Curriculum IT Support Projects which it funds, and NCET manages, to assess the availability and quality of software for key stages 1-4 and to highlight any gaps in the current provision. The Geography IT Support Project which is jointly managed by the Geographical Association (GA) and NCET carried out the review. The activity was based on initial research of the available software using up-to-date information and was supported by interviews and by members of the Geographical Association Information Technology Working Group (GA ITWG), the teacher training community, NCET, OFSTED and a number of other experts.

Much of the geography software available which was reviewed has been produced by small companies or subsidiaries of educational publishing houses that sell directly to schools. The majority of software to support our geography curriculum is developed in the UK, although atlases and encyclopaedias are, for the most part, from the USA. About 80 subject-specific software titles that cover geography at key stage 3 and key stage 4 have been scrutinised, two-thirds of which are only available on CD-ROM. The majority of these titles cover both key stage 3 and key stage 4 and are in the ratio of three for PC to two for Acorn and one for Apple Macintosh.

What types of geographical learning are covered?

The findings on the learning types and themes in the software are summarised in Table 1.

Type of learning	Percentage of software
Data logging	4
Enquiry	35
Exam study	1
Interpretation	31
INSET	1
Knowledge	32
Mapping	11
Simulation	1

By geographical theme	Percentage of software
Development	11
Economic activities	25
Ecosystems	8
Environment	27
Geomorphology	11
Population	20
Settlement	15
Skills	44
Tectonics	8
Weather and climate	23

Table 1: Geographical software by type of learning and by geographical theme.

Content-rich resources

The overwhelming majority of the titles (89 per cent) for the secondary phase are content-based. Geographical images and information provide the basis for colourful, well-presented visual materials that are appealing, although many have serious limitations for classroom use. These titles present their contents in three main ways:

- as an image bank with picture captions and a search mechanism (30 per cent);
- as statistical data with a interrogation program and possibly map representation (33 per cent);
- an electronic book of images and explanations of specific topics or places, often divided into 'chapters' with a narrative (28 per cent).

All of these require a strong lead from the teacher as the materials rarely have enough guidance for students. The best have worksheets or activities for students which are sometimes within the software. Some provide guidance for teachers on learning opportunities and methods and the organisation and management of classes. Those produced for the 'edu-tainment' market (about 20 per cent) do not have any educational support materials.

Skill-based resources

Only eleven of the programs analysed deal directly with geographical skills. They may be divided into two categories: collecting and analysing remotely-sensed data, and mapping programs. Others deal with the more generic skills of information handling, communicating and presenting information.

Collecting and analysing remotely-sensed data

1. **Local data** - Many schools are using an automatic data-logging weather station to provide continuous local weather data for analysis by students and hand-held data-logging devices are used to a lesser extent to gather environmental data in the field.

2. **Global data** - There is a small number of weather satellite-receiving systems for collecting current images from NOAA and Meteosat weather satellites. However, schools also use alternative methods, such as the Meteorological Office MetFAX service or the World Wide Web, to obtain the images. Remotely-sensed data on land cover from Landsat and other satellites is available in limited quantities, although there are few materials that enable teacher and students to understand the processing or interpretation of images.

Mapping programs

Map skills are an essential part of the geographer's art. Although a number of content-rich programs present information on maps, there is only a small number that help students understand and practise mapping skills. However, map skills programs tend to be limited in both geographical content and their use of IT.

Most of the available atlases are of US origin and of very variable quality. The UK is not well represented on these atlases.

Geographical information systems (GIS) provide the tools for the spatial analysis of geographic data from local to global scales. They can support high-order geographic and IT skills and require teacher mediation to maximise their undoubted potential. LEA schools gain access to Ordnance Survey digital maps through their local authority, and

Grant Maintained and independent schools may buy these maps at an educational rate. There are very few products targeted at schools and there is a lack of knowledge and experience in schools about how digital maps can enhance and extend students' geographical skills.

Simulations and modelling resources

This area of geographical learning is inadequately resourced. The simulations produced in the early phase of subsidised educational software development in the UK have not been updated. There is evidence that these packages were used as they fitted the curriculum, had useful teaching materials and were able to be used effectively within one lesson by teachers with little computer experience. Simulations cannot by their nature extend students' use of ICT to the higher levels, but there is scope to move on to more open-ended generic modelling tools which have geographical examples and data. There is a lack of both simulation and modelling materials for geography.

Representation of places

Most titles present statistical data on all countries of the world (46 per cent) or UK data and resources (38 per cent). Japan (3), USA (1), W Africa (1), E Africa (3) and countries of Europe (4) are all represented, while other more general resources may have case studies of different localities. There is inadequate coverage of all countries at key stage 3 – only Japan has been addressed in any detail, and detailed IT resources for Europe, Russian Federation, South and Central America, most of Africa, Australia and New Zealand are practically non-existent. However, the Internet may provide first-hand resources directly from the countries in question.

Coverage of geographical themes

Coverage of the nine key stage 3 and 4 themes in available software is outlined in the following list:

ICT

- **Tectonic processes**
  About six CD-ROMs cover the theme of earthquakes and volcanoes, with some 'edu-tainment' disks. There is a shortage of interactive materials to help students fully understand the processes, but Internet resources are available to support this theme.
- **Geomorphological processes**
  Basic resources are found in eight CD-ROMs (only one on glaciation), but again there is insufficient interactive student involvement to gain understanding of the processes.
- **Weather and climate**
  Around 17 titles provide resource materials on weather and climate. The Internet is a worldwide resource for up-to-date climate and weather data, including recent satellite images.
- **Ecosystems**
  Ecosystems are not the main focus of any CD-ROM, but the theme is supported in a number of general ways in conjunction with others.
- **Population**
  This is mainly represented by statistical data on countries or regions within a country. Fifteen disks provide information on population, but not the causes and effects of population change.
- **Economic activities**
  Economic activities are covered on disks which have statistical data for countries of the world. Specific themes, such as farming, industry and transport, are not well represented.
- **Settlement**
  Settlement is poorly represented.
- **Environmental issues**
  Although environment is represented in a reasonable number of disks (20), the nature and type of issues do not sufficiently address the demands of the geography curriculum.
- **Development**
  Of the small number of disks (8), some are narratives on localities and are produced by aid agencies, while the rest offer statistical data on countries of the world.

How can software enhance the quality of geographical learning?

Software which gives the greatest potential for learning offers a high degree of student interaction and flexibility. Students should be able to manipulate and analyse information from a variety of sources, such as using weather or statistical data; interpreting photographs; writing reports; presenting a case for role-play with pictures from CD-ROMs or the Internet; or saving time by drawing and analysing graphs, diagrams or maps on computer.

The following advice is offered to teachers:

1. Write your own support material
Although there are good CD-ROMs, feedback from teachers suggests that the majority of 'electronic book' CD-ROMs are restrictive. There are a few that have activities within the CD-ROM, but they do not necessarily address the required geographical issues or concepts. Some teachers reported that they write their own materials to extend students' learning with these disks.

2. Share experiences
It would be helpful if there was a recognised, comprehensive, current list of available geography software for teachers, but in the short term teachers should try to share good and bad experiences so each department does not reinvent the wheel.

3. Inspect before purchase
Try to look at CD-ROMs and software before you buy; only a very few publishers offer inspection copies of software titles, though it is always worth asking for them.

4. Have access to a tool kit
There are gaps in provision and improvements that could be made in the products for teaching geography with IT. One thing departments could do is to ensure they have access to all the tools they need. The investigation suggests that the best approach would be to define an IT 'tool kit' for all schools teaching secondary geography.

The tool kit should contain:
Generic software packages – already available in most schools

- Word-processor; database; spreadsheet; desk-top publishing package; multimedia authoring tools.
- Internet browser for access to current, dynamic resources on the World Wide Web, and associated e-mail facilities.

Geography software and data

- Quality CD-ROM electronic atlas and encyclopaedia.
- Modelling software (quantitative and qualitative).
- Geographical information system (GIS) with digital map data.
- Automatic data-logging weather station.
- Map and statistical data for local and place studies.

While packages exist which could help to fill this 'tool kit', some are lacking. These include graphing population pyramids from spreadsheets and databases; more flexible modelling software; more quality UK-centric atlases; appropriate fully-functional GIS packages and access to digital map data; better quality CD-ROMs targeted at key places and themes with appropriate curriculum support materials. ■

Information

BECTa are currently working for the DfEE in reviewing and updating this report on the quality and availability of educational software. Further information will appear (during 2000) on the BECTa website: www.becta.org.uk.

For further information on reviewing CD-ROMs, look at the software review section over the past year in *Teaching Geography*, or the 'Computer update' section of the *Times Educational Supplement* (June 1997, p. 28).

Diana Freeman is on the IT Working Group and chairs its GIS sub-group. She works for the Advisory Unit Computers in Education, Hatfield.

Software and hardware

7 CD-ROM technology in geography: potential and issues

Photo: Andrew Williams.

Helen Warner offers some advice on using CD-ROMS in the classroom

There is enormous potential for enhancing geography with a range of resources that can be put on a CD-ROM disk. Such resources can include map reading skills, exploring landscapes, views of distant places, simulations and geographical case studies.

CD-ROM technology has only recently (1994) reached the average classroom, and the growth of titles has mushroomed over the last year. However, there is little research on how this resource can affect and enhance learning.

Content

After reviewing 28 geography titles, I was struck by the lack of good material. In particular, content was not always matched to the national curriculum, nor was it always appropriate, free from bias or interesting.

One compact disk I reviewed contains lots of satellite images. As a geography teacher, I might, for instance, wish to look at deforestation evidence from the satellite images. However, only one image matched this enquiry and the associated explanation was brief and of limited value. I investigated other themes with similar disappointment. The disk is a collection of images, particularly from the USA, for which copyright is available. I am not suggesting that this disk is not useful; however, without a clear reason for using such a resource, students could passively browse through the material with limited learning gains.

There are several disks where the USA bias in content coverage is evident. Teachers need to be aware of possible inaccuracies and bias. For example, on one comprehensive world atlas disk, a search on Aids cases displays none in North America or Europe. I also looked at the information held on my home area, Greenwich; this was full of spatial inaccuracies. There is a danger, particularly with computer media, that content can be read without question as fact.

The language on disks should be appropriate for the students who will be using them. One useful global statistics data disk contains information from the *Third World Almanac*. The articles come directly from academic journals - suitable for A-level groups, but not for general classroom use.

Content can also affect how students use the disk. Some disks contain screens with multiple-choice questions, with some help or support given if the student gets the answer wrong - a random clicking ensues. Disks which encourage passivity, with no useful feedback, are likely to be of limited value.

Some initial questions about content could therefore include:

- Is there an appropriate mix of text, images, sound, video, etc., and are they of high quality?

- Is the content relevant to the curriculum?
- Are the content and activities appropriate for your student?
- Are the support materials provided of high quality?
- Does the CD-ROM provide value for money?

(Hassell, 1997, p. 95).

The issue of browsing

There is now enough research evidence on using hyper-media which shows that browsing in itself is not a useful learning strategy. Browsing can quickly become an activity where students fail to see the main thrust of an enquiry and are led into a passive role; learning is likely to be reduced in these circumstances, particularly amongst the least able.

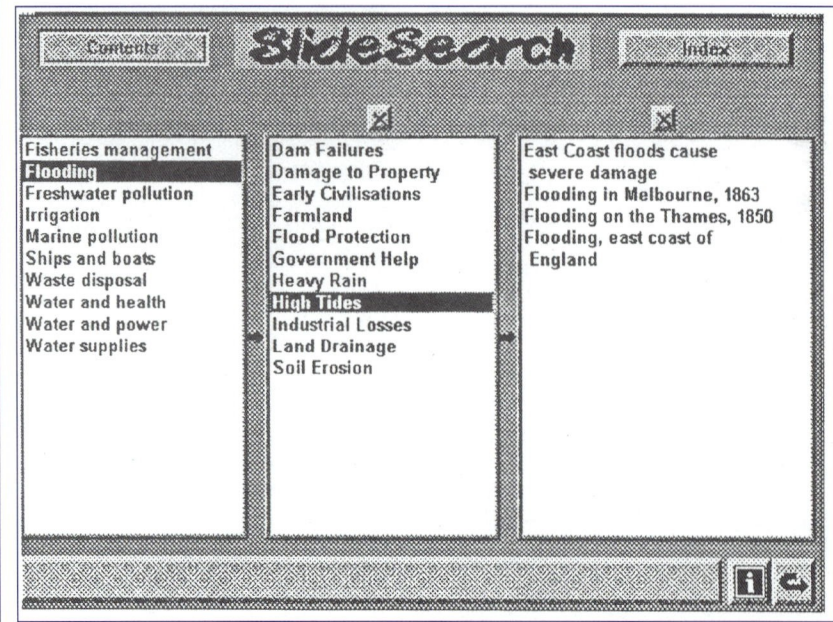

Figure 1: A clear method of searching from *Environment – Water*, Academy TV.

Students need clear tasks, not necessarily closed tasks, because there are such vast amounts of information stored on a CD-ROM. It is easy to digress into some interesting alternative but potentially irrelevant avenue. In this respect, using a CD-ROM has been likened to going round a museum, wandering off and getting lost! It is easy to be information-rich but knowledge-poor. Thus the teacher needs to plan for educational outcomes when using a CD-ROM resource, as with any other resource.

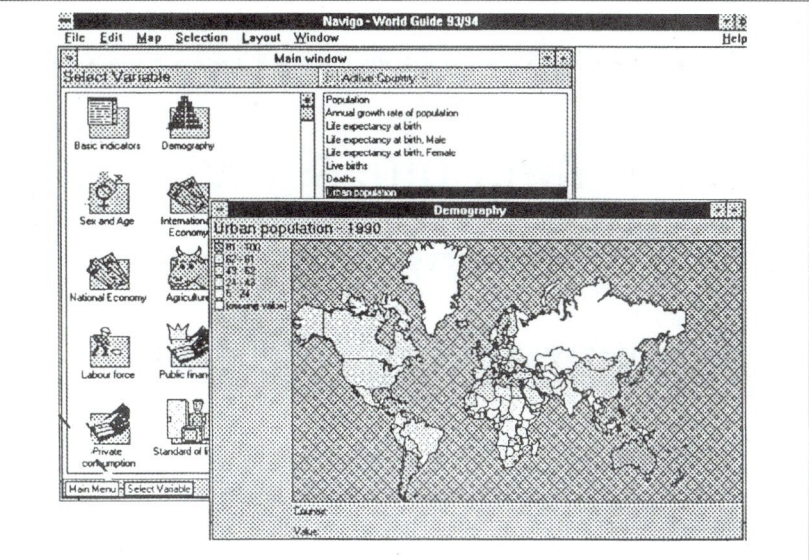

Figure 2: Access to information from a useful icon menu page. The main navigation route through the disk is via the bottom bar. *Navigo World Guide 93/94.*

Design and navigation

The key issue with design is the way the user searches out information and 'navigates' a way around the content. A teacher might need to consider a number of questions about the design of a CD-ROM:

- Will it run on the type(s) of computer(s) in your school or college?
- Is it easy to use?
- Is a method for searching provided, and is it easy to use?
- Can you store or mark useful information for later use?
- Can you print, copy and save the contents?

(Hassell, 1997, p. 95).

Recent NCET research

Some recent research sponsored by NCET (now BECTa) looked at the schools which piloted work on CD-ROMs. Findings suggested that:

- Students take to the medium quickly.
- Students demonstrate confidence in exploring the medium.
- 60 per cent of teachers responding noted positive effect on students attitudes to search and enquiry, and increased self-motivation.
- CD-ROMS were equally attractive to girls and boys.
- Most effective use came where the teacher acted as a guide or joint interpreter of information.

The positive effects on students' attitudes to search and enquiry is an important finding for geography teachers. Enquiry underpins good geography, and a medium which can enhance enquiry method may have great potential in geography. The research suggests that students need opportunities for:

- learning through reflection in small groups which share responsibility for a single outcome, rather than direct teaching of search skills;
- looking critically at information on disks.

The most successful use of CD-ROMs took place when teachers:

- provide opportunities for, and teach students how, to refine their search skills;
- teach students how to skim through a mass of information to identify relevant pieces;
- plan for differentiation, by matching tasks to abilities, by expecting different outcomes, or providing differing amounts of support;
- provide opportunities so that sections from CD-ROMs can be incorporated into other applications.

The pilot study also revealed that location was often a barrier to use and that successful use depends upon the existence of a school policy which promotes CD-ROM as a whole-school resource, with systems located within subject base areas.

CD-ROM technology should be able to enhance learning. My own personal request is for simulation-type titles to be developed: titles which enable students to explore the impact of developments and changes on landscapes and environments. I would like to see educational titles developed which enable students to visit distant places and get a balanced, interactive view of life in these places. We also need publishers to listen to teachers' needs, consider good design principles, and trial materials before publication. ■

Benefits for learning

- Is it flexible and will it support differentiation?
- How will you actually use the product with your students?
- Will it engage your students?
- What does the CD-ROM provide that other formats cannot?

(Hassell, 1997, p. 95).

Editor's note

Although one of the oldest texts in this collection, much of what is written here remains valid. The number of CD-ROMs available has risen significantly in the last five years, yet few are interactive or offer an innovative use of the multimedia medium.

Reference

Hassell, D. (1997) 'New resources (CD-ROMs checklist)', *Teaching Geography*, 22, 2, p. 95.

Helen Warner is ICT adviser for the London Borough of Tower Hamlets.

Software and hardware

8 Something old, something new, something borrowed – and something 'off the Internet'

David Hassell takes a look at the Geography IT Support Project and some ideas which can be adopted from a sister project

The Geography and IT Support Project has now been running for four years (1994-98) with funding from the Department for Education and Employment (DfEE). The Project produces materials and encourages in-service training (INSET) and other activities to support geography teachers in developing the use of information and communications technology (ICT) to enhance the teaching and learning of geography. Over the lifetime of the Project, a number of materials have been produced, starting with the Entitlement leaflets which was sent to all English maintained schools. This was followed by a series of three packs with good ideas for developing the use of ICT in themes within the curriculum that all geography teachers cover. The most recent publication is a departmental planning booklet which builds on the Entitlement leaflet and provides geography staff with essential support and guidance for developing and implementing their ICT policy.

Project activities

The Geography and IT Project continues to support local INSET providers with a CD-ROM roadshow which has been enhanced with further materials and activities. If you do not have the opportunity to evaluate CD-ROMs, ask your LEA or INSET provider to apply for the pack; it does not cost the centre anything to borrow the materials. If you are interested in reviews of CD-ROMs, these can be accessed through the Project web pages on the BECTa website: vtc.ngfl.gov.uk/resource/cits/geog

In 1994 and 1995, the Project produced entitlement leaflets for both primary and secondary schools *(Primary Geography: a student's entitlement to IT* and *Geography: a student's entitlement for IT,* respectively). This year, the Project is developing a guide which elaborates on the planning cycle and provides starting-points and, produced in 1999, a free planning booklet for key stage 2 teachers wishing to integrate the use of ICT into their geography curriculum.

The Internet

The Internet has huge potential for geographers and much of the year's activities are linked to the Project's website (Figure 1) and how it can be developed. It is hoped that this will become a self-sustaining focus for good practice, both in relation to the Internet and the use of ICT in general. It is envisaged that the Project will continue to provide material for the site, but the expectation is that teachers and other professionals will increasingly be able to contribute. As a basis for this there are a number of different elements which are being developed over the year:

1. Last year's pages have been updated with the news, Entitlement documents and CD-ROM reviews.
2. An area is being developed to provide a forum for disseminating good practice in the use of ICT. A number of case studies are being provided as a starting-point; these include background information, a description and sample files which can be downloaded. The first three examples are on using ICT in 'Industrial location', 'River studies' and 'Atlas work'. However, the main aim is to provide a space for you to contribute and share successful geography and ICT classroom practice.

Another element of this work is the development of some activities from ICT-based geographical models. We all work with many abstract ideas or with data and information, and often like to reassess our ideas from different angles. Computer-based models provide students with access to a dynamic version of a concept, such as a model of part of the water cycle, or the opportunity to investigate different perspectives of a decision-making process. The Geography and IT Project is developing case studies with down loadable files, which will be placed on the website to provide teachers with some starting-points and ideas on how computer models can enhance geography teaching and learning.

3. Many people think of World Wide Web pages when the Internet is mentioned. This is, however, only one aspect of the Internet. A joint initiative between the Project and the University of Leeds School of Education is investigating the effective use of the Internet in geography. From this research it is hoped that a number of case studies and other information will appear on the Project website. There may also be activities organised during spring term 1998. For details of current activities, visit the website.

4. Related to this work, the Project has been working with a series of people to provide reviews of a wide range of websites. Reviews of a number of websites can already be found on the Project website, and if you look at a site which has not been reviewed, please consider evaluating it. The Project website has an on-line evaluation form which can be completed and e-mailed to Dave Hassell, or you can print it, complete a paper copy and mail it to BECTa.

Borrowing good ideas

The Geography IT Support Project is one of eleven projects which the DfEE has been supporting over the last four years. Each Project's remit is to look at how ICT can enhance the teaching and learning of the subject, and most have worked in quite different directions. However, there are lots of good ideas in one subject area which are appropriate in most, if not all, other subjects. Geography has concentrated on data handling and so the use of a word-processor has received little discussion. Many departments use word-processing and desktop-publishing software simply as a tool for writing up their coursework or fieldwork. Unfortunately, some follow the (poor) practice where students type their best copy having completed any writing by hand.

In my view, word-processing/desktop-publishing software should be seen as a tool which provides a range of opportunities for improving the processes in which students are working. One common activity is the use of writing frames which allow teachers to provide differentiated tasks for students. Some have more support for the weaker students and others encourage well-structured extended writing (Jones *et al.*, 1997). Below are a series of one-off ideas which teachers can use in a wide variety of contexts, all of which make use of the basic (non-specific) word-processing facilities on your system.

Accessing text

Present the students with a section of word-processed text on screen. Omit all headings, sub-headings, bullet points, line spacing, etc. Give different groups or pairs the following challenges:

1. Highlight key words and phrases that need explaining, and create a glossary using a thesaurus or dictionary.
2. Add a main heading and any appropriate sub-headings.
3. Change the layout of the text to make it easier to understand by adding bullet points, italics, line spacing, etc.
4. Choose two pictures from other sources to accompany the extract and add references to them, explaining why these pictures were chosen.
5. Add short questions to help the reader reflect on and review the information given in the text.
6. Students print the amendments and orally explain their choices either in groups or to the whole class.

Encourage them to explain:

- what they considered were the significant issues;
- how they decided to convey these messages to the reader; and
- how doing this exercise will help them to use other text-based sources.

Both CD-ROMs and the Internet are a good source of text-based materials, but if you are using text from these sources, **please remember copyright considerations.**

Selecting information

Present the students with some word-processed text (on screen). They should study this text, which is then followed by a question (again on screen).

1. Ask them to highlight any words and phrases which they feel have something to do with the question.
2. Using the cut and paste facility, get the students to arrange the information in bullet points beneath the question.
3. They should delete any extracts which duplicate each other (making sure that one statement remains!).
4. Finally, they can weave the statements into an answer. To do this, students must add link words/phrases/sentences to make a fluent answer.

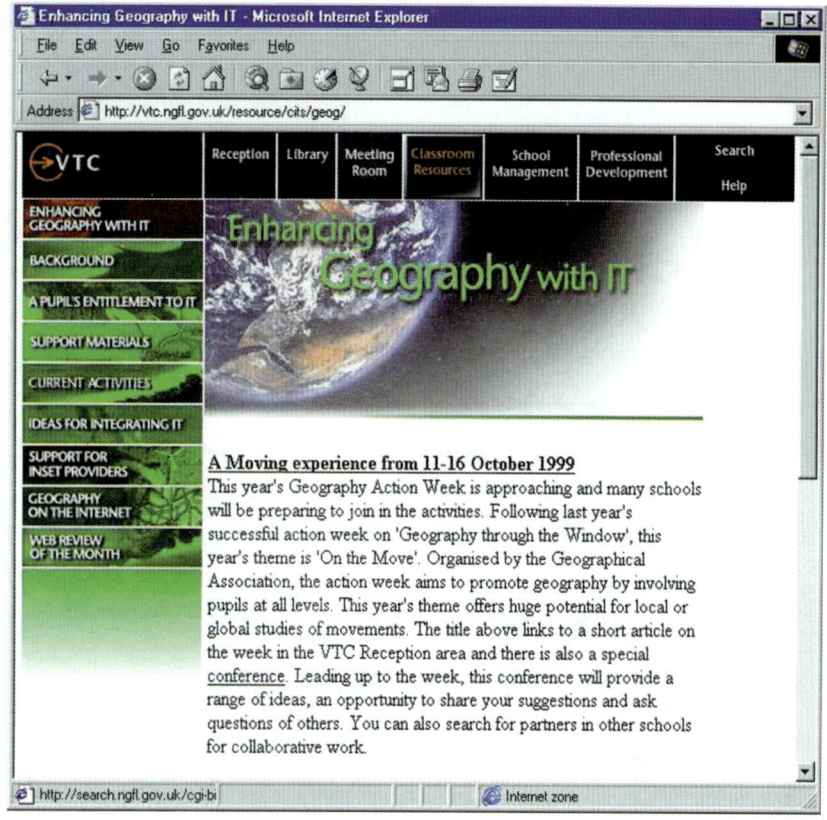

Figure 1: The Geography and IT Support Project website.

Sorting and setting

On a word-processor, provide students with a pre-prepared list of reasons for a decision to place an industry in a particular location, or some other issue.

1. Ask the students to highlight the social, physical, economic and political reasons, using a different font for each. Alternatively, ask students to attribute the statements to different interest groups in an issue.
2. Get the students to cut and paste their chosen reasons into sets.
3. Ask them to put the reasons in rank order of importance, if possible, and be prepared to justify the order.
4. If some reasons fall into more than one category, ask students to explain why this is.

Interpreting sources

On a word-processor, present the students with an account of an issue they are studying. Ask groups or pairs of students to highlight, using a different font or italics, phrases or words in the text which:

- show key facts about the issue;
- need further explanation;
- indicate the attitude of the author to the issue;
- show the intended audience;
- suggest that the information may be subjective or generalised.

Print the highlighted versions and draw the ideas together in a whole-class discussion. The aim of this exercise is to reach some conclusions about the source and evaluate it in relation to the topic being studied.

These examples were abstracted from work produced by Gillian Temple, the history adviser in Devon for the History and IT Project. If you teach history as well as geography, you may find the publication from which these ideas come a very useful purchase (see below). ■

Further information

History Using IT: Improving student's writing with a word-processor (price £15.00) provides a wealth of practical ideas, further details are available from BECTa.
More details of the Geography IT Support Project can be found at website: vtc.ngfl.gov.uk/resource/cits/geog or from David Hassell (address below).

Reference
Jones, B., Swift, D. and Vickers, D. (1997) 'Writing about development', *Teaching Geography*, 22, 1, pp. 5-10.

David Hassell is Head of Curriculum and Institutional Development for Schools, British Educational Communications and Technology Agency (BECTa); e-mail: david_hassell@becta.org.uk

Software and hardware

9 Geographers on the Internet

Chris Durbin and **Roger Sanders** introduce the opportunities presented by the information revolution

The use of the Internet in the UK is now taking off. Estimates of the number of schools and colleges connected to the Internet range between 2000 and 3000 and the numbers may double by the end of the year (1996). However, the Internet is only just beginning to have an impact in schools, let alone geography classrooms.

BBC Education, together with the National Council for Educational Technology (now BECTa), has been running a pilot project to investigate the emerging application of global networks of computers and we have drawn on the findings of that project in writing this article. Our aim here is to introduce you to the opportunities presented by the Internet for the teaching and learning of geography, and to urge a rational approach at this stage of development.

What is the Internet?

The Internet is not the so-called 'Information Superhighway'; this will only be in place when video can be transferred by computer networks as easily as it is over the airwaves today. The Internet is a network of computer networks which started in the USA, but the spider's web of inter-connectivity now extends all over the world. Nobody owns it; nobody oversees it; but people and organisations can see its benefits and anyone can participate in it if they have a telephone, a modem, a computer, and a membership or a link to the Internet. Teachers have been aware of e-mail for some time but it has been the ease of access of World Wide Web that has enabled people to see and realise the potential for education.

Internet services

The main Internet services which are of interest to geographers are:

- World Wide Web – enables you to view and browse through text, photographs and graphics, including maps (and audio and video material, although this is very slow and impractical unless you have a powerful computer).

- Electronic mail (e-mail) – enables you to communicate quickly and easily with others across the globe. This is particularly useful for people involved in the study of geography, and those engaged in studying places and issues.

- File transfer (FTP) – enables you to transfer large amounts of unseen information from another computer to your own. Using this, it is possible to move video files, such as an animated passage about a hurricane.

- Newsgroups – these are e-mail discussion and help groups. Experts on geographical information systems (GIS) have a discussion group, for example.

What does the Internet offer?

BBC Education created a series of World Wide Web pages designed to encourage geography teachers to begin to explore the Internet for use in the classroom. The unique characteristics of this technology compared with other media, such as video, audio and CD-ROM, are only just becoming apparent. The following are areas where the Internet is very valuable, and in some cases unique.

Hazard events

The Internet offers up-to-the minute information about some events that have made an impact in the news. After three or four days, hazard events are no longer newsworthy, so information about them is difficult to find. This is when the Internet becomes a very useful tool. Information about the Kobe earthquake, for example, is still available on the Internet from the City of Kobe Council (Figure 1). Television news carried stories about the earthquake for just over seven days, but these nearly always focused on Britons abroad. The Internet, on the other hand, provided an opportunity to communicate with ordinary citizens of Kobe. This included 8 to 19-year-olds in two schools – Akayatsuyama High School (Figure 2) and Nada Elementary School. There is no doubt that a video of the news conveys the drama of a sudden unexpected tragedy, but the Internet

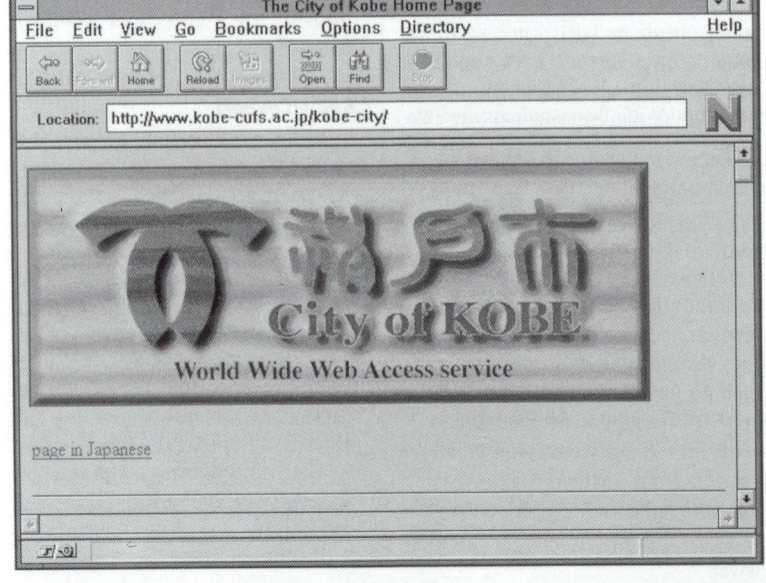

Figure 1: Kobe City Home Page (www.city.kobe.jp/) This page originally provided the links to data and images of the earthquake and to schools in Kobe.

provides a more considered environment in which to access the latest information. It takes time for the full impact of a natural hazard to unfold and for full details to be revealed. Internet users have been able to access pictures (Figure 3) and statistics (Figure 4) every day since the Kobe earthquake. They have also been able to participate themselves by communicating directly with people involved and joining in on their planning for reconstruction projects.

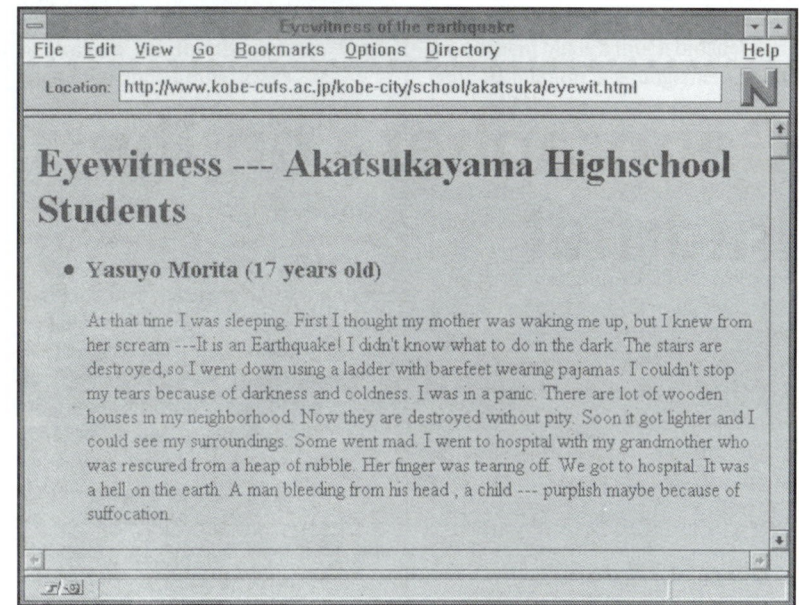

Figure 2: Eyewitness from Akayatsuyama High School. This is one moving account from students of the High School and Nada Elementary School.

Internet gobbledygook

Many people are intimidated by jargon, most of which is unnecessary. Don't be! You simply need to know the most important terms, such as those set out below:

URL is the Uniform Resource Locator which is just a unique page 'filename' like an address of where a page is found. In practice, you may never need it, but it can save you time. For example: www.sln.org.uk will transport you to the web pages of Staffordshire LEA's geography site. The URL is nearly always in lower case and there are no spaces between letters or symbols. Here are the meanings of some abbreviations:

com or co – commercial
org – non profit-making organisation
edu or ac – educational or academic
gov – government
uk – United Kingdom
jp – Japan
za – South Africa
au – Australia
Note: US sites have no country abbreviation

Pages on the World Wide Web are constantly changing. The addresses (URLs) can also change. The authors apologise if readers experience difficulties in accessing websites; if you do, you should use an Internet Searcher and put in key words.

Data on demand

The Internet is unique because it offers users cheap and easy access to so much information - the USA Census data is freely available, for example. On the World Wide Web, students are able to fill in an interactive application form. Imagine the scenario: you have just watched the video *USA 2000* about Los Angeles (BBC Education, 1995). A student asks a question for which you do not have the information available. You find the 'US Census Lookup' (Figure 5), choose the place coverage, then the type of data, and within minutes (in the morning) direct from the USA comes information such as percentage of Hispanic origin or percentage in different social groups. This data is available 'on demand'. You could get the book or visit the library, or you could access the data when you need it, usually for the cost of a local phone call *(tariffs depend on the location of your Internet connection and the time of day)*.

The provenance of data and information varies enormously. National governments, big companies and individuals are all providing data for different purposes. Often, some of the best World Wide Web 'sites' are those set up by people simply for the 'love of it'. The pages Bem-Vindo Ao Brasil (darkwing.uoregon.edu/~sergiok/brasil.html) have been created by a Brazilian professor at the University of Oregon. This site includes a great deal of geographical information, maps and pictures relating to Brazil. In the UK, the CTI Centre for Geography, Geology and Meteorology (www.le.ac.uk/cti/), based at the University of Leicester, is a great starting-point.

Using the Internet, you need never be short of information, assuming of course that it has been collected. Students will even be able to update your textbooks for you!

Ask an expert

Being able to consult an expert is another valuable feature of the Internet. This is best illustrated by *Volcano World* (Figure 6), a site produced at the University of North Dakota. Scott Rowland and Chuck Morris, vulcanologists, answer your questions about vulcanology and the questions asked are stored as 'frequently or previously asked' questions. Such access means that students and their parents can find answers to homework with responses usually being returned within a few days! You will receive your personal e-mail but it is also posted for the benefit of others (Figure 7). If Scott and Chuck cannot answer a question, they will pass it on to another academic who should be able to. When you come to ask your own questions, make sure you check the 'previously-asked questions' so that you do not waste the experts' time!

On-line fieldwork

The Jason Project (no longer available) was an indicator of the possibilities for the future. Although largely aimed at young scientists, it enabled students to interact with scientists collecting information in the field. They were able to pose questions to researchers and receive responses. In the future this could happen 'live' - a hint of the superhighway potential. Here is a possible scenario:

'Students arrive at 9.25 a.m. on Monday morning for a geography lesson. They log on to their computer, check the time in Malaysia, call up the XIth Jason Project and encounter an interactive map of the archive and live locations and journeys available for that day. They choose a journey being made by a researcher in the rainforest in real time and they choose the camera that follows the researcher. They may ask the researcher questions about the environment that they move through.'

Author's note (1999)

Virtual fieldwork has yet to develop 'live' websites, but websites that may prove of interest do exist, for example: http://www.stromboli.ch
Web cams (video cameras linked live to a website) such as 'Peeping Tom' (www.coolbase.com/peepingtom/index.html) can bring distant places straight into the classroom.

Figure 3: Kobe earthquake. Hundreds of images were available on demand. The collapsed expressway was one example.

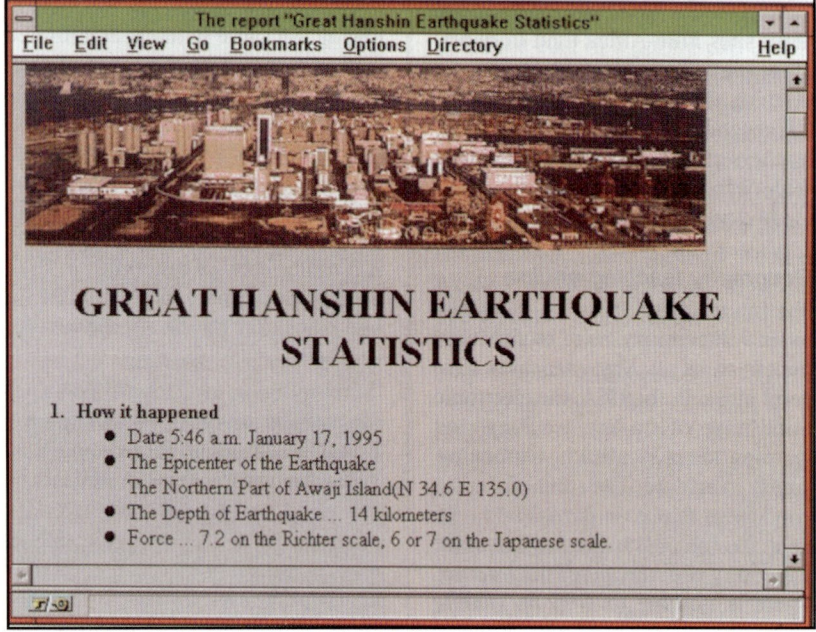

Figure 4: Sample of the Great Hanshin earthquake statistics. Below this introductory information were four pages of data on the impact and cost of the earthquake.

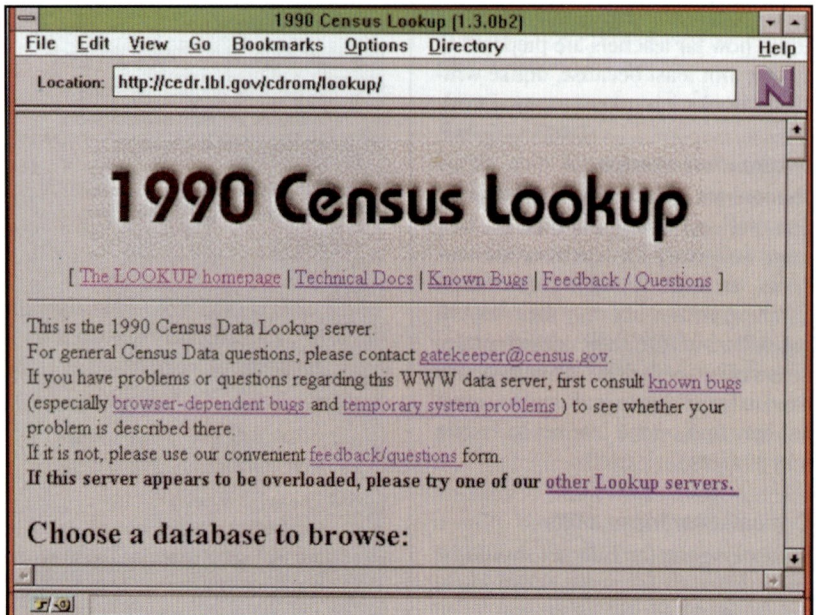

Figure 5: The USA Census Lookup Home Page. The US Census Bureau (www.census.gov) contains up-to-date census data.

Figure 6: Volcano World (volcano.und.nodak.edu/). This interactive maps and pictures of hundreds of volcanoes

The global classroom

The Internet is unique in being able to link your classroom with others around the world. The World Wide Web enables you to introduce yourselves and to meet other students studying geography, and other teachers teaching it. Schools and teachers are 'on line'. For example, Low Bentham County Primary School, near Lancaster (cres1.lancs.ac.uk), has its own 'locality study' for the rest of the world to view. The Atlas of Canadian Communities Project (Figure 8) is a collection of local history and geography studies developed by students in Canadian schools. These can be accessed via a 'clickable' map.

Thus the global classroom is an emerging possibility. George Thornton, a geography and social studies teacher in Oroville, USA, was introduced to geography in the UK. He sent an e-mail saying he wished to share geography teaching and learning experiences with UK schools. Immediately, this message was passed to 50 schools. At Sir John Talbot School in Whitchurch, Shropshire, it was decided that this could add to the learning experiences of students in geography. Dialogue began with a discussion about the sort of projects that would be most beneficial. With the relative ease and cheapness of communication between staff and students, perspectives on aspects of geography will be shared and discussed. Sharing perceptions of each other's countries will be an excellent starting-point.

In studying environmental issues, perspectives from localities all over the world will be drawn in. In an enquiry about air pollution, for example, information from your own locality could be swapped with many other localities. Remember, the Internet is not the Information Superhighway: it is more like an 'information A-road in the

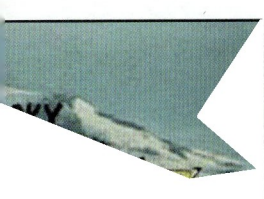

sponsored by NASA and has a fantastic array of data, ...hout the world.

1960s' along which text will pass very efficiently and still pictures transfer at a reasonable rate. Eventually, the capability to exchange video documentaries about your own locality will enable a whole new range of teaching and learning strategies to emerge.

There are sites for higher education on the Internet that encourage live participation. For example, you can join 'live' in virtual classrooms and participate in discussions about a subject you are interested in. Whilst this is unique and realistic for a few people who work at their desktops, it is still unrealistic for the classroom. Global students, in striving to make sense of the world, will, as a matter of course, look for and find other perspectives on many aspects of their work.

What are the emerging issues?

Do not be afraid of this technology. While it can be frustrating, there should be no difficulty in understanding the relatively simple way it works. If you are accustomed to using 'point and click', with a mouse, then the World Wide Web offers no real barriers. Some issues remain unresolved, such as technical reliability and funding, and these are not dealt with here because there are so many different variables and costs. It is best for people to investigate for themselves.

Some issues relating to teaching and learning in geography, are beginning to emerge, as discussed below.

Developing world data

New technologies are in the hands of the rich nations: it is they who are embracing them. There are many fewer sites from Africa than from any other part of the world. Even so, for teaching about developing countries in UK geography, it should be possible for teachers and students to create World Wide Web information and sites relat-

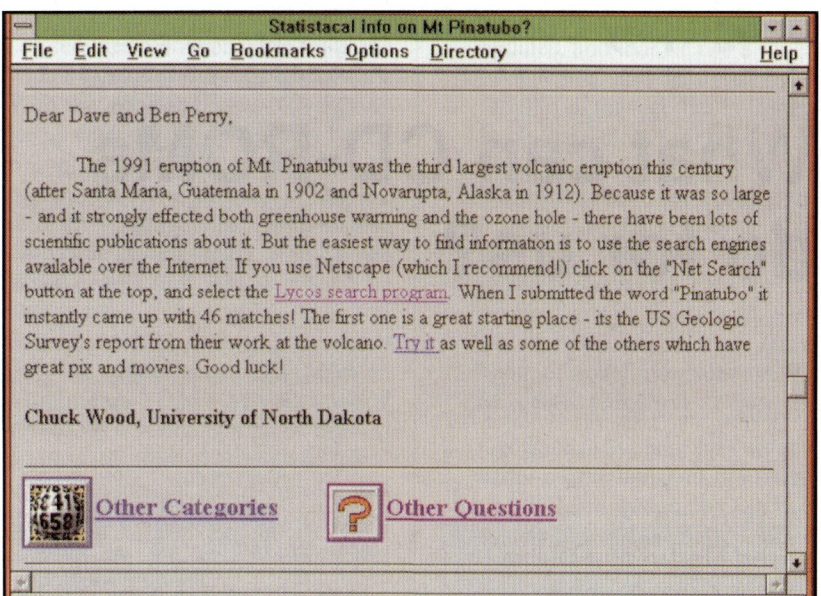

Figure 7: Answer to a frequently-asked question from Volcano World. (volcano.und.nodak.edu/vwdocs/ask_a.html). The question was: 'My son is doing a project on Mount Pinatubo for grade II geography. Could you help him find some information?'.

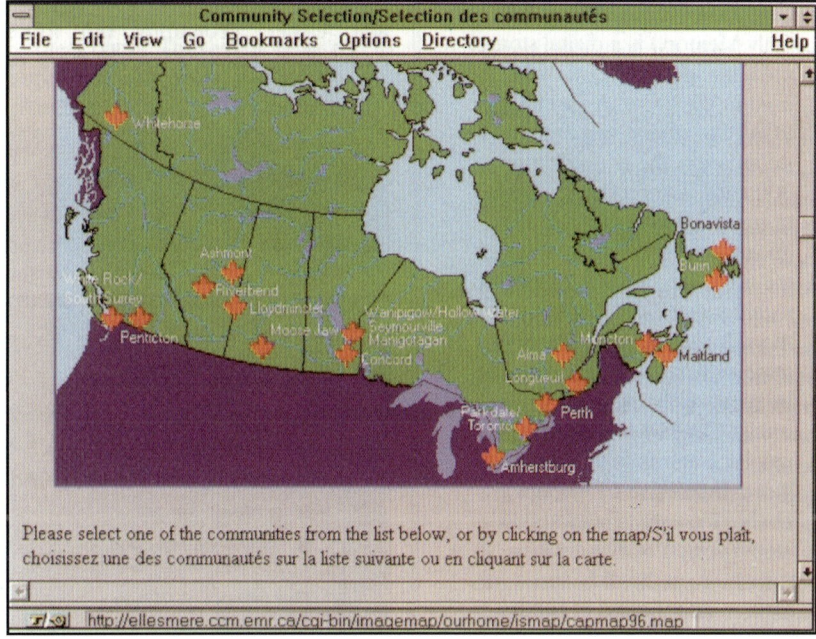

Figure 8: The Atlas of Canadian Communities Project (ellesmere.ccm.emr.ca/ourhome/ourhome/selectio.html) is a 'clickable' map. Behind each little maple leaf is a collection of local geographical study, often this has been provided by a school.

ing to development issues. One World on-line: www.oneworld.org is a notable exception.

Geography teaching on-line

Sharing teaching ideas, on a mutual basis, will certainly be of professional benefit to us all. Many teachers have good ideas. In the USA, the electronic publishing of on-line teaching and learning ideas is already happening. The spirit of sharing good ideas may have diminished a little in the UK of late, but it could make a recovery with the aid of the Internet. There is nothing to stop us sharing ideas with geography teachers in Australia, for example. Geography Teachers Association of Victoria is now online (www.netspace.net.au/~gtav). The issue is really about how far teachers are prepared to do this, not least because, unlike writing textbooks, it is unremunerated work. (Editor's note: Staffordshire Learning Net Geography Teachers' site is a new example: www.sln.org.uk/geography.)

Information overload

The Internet contributes to an information-overload society and makes it even more necessary for teachers and students to improve their information-handling skills - not only their searching skills, but also their critical-awareness skills (see below). They will also need to learn how to evaluate the material they find on the Internet to ensure that it meets their needs.

Critical-awareness skills

Students using the Internet should be encouraged to ask these questions of the material they will encounter:

- What is the provenance of the information?
- How reliable is it?
- What is the motive for publishing the information electronically?
- Are there other perspectives that could be developed?

A sign that students have developed critical awareness will be when, having accessed a commercial or an environmentalist's page on the Internet, they think about, and search for, other opinions and/or other evidence.

In summary, the development of critical-awareness skills is a major priority for teachers and students who are using the Internet.

Teaching and learning opportunities

The use of a textbook is viewed by many teachers as a safe refuge and means of control, with all students following the same path, as determined by the teacher. With the Internet, multiple-learning outcomes are possible from the same geographical investigation, and the range of perspectives and places that can be accessed will be unlimited. The benefit, of course, will be that students will realise that there is a multiplicity of outcomes in their investigations and what is suitable for one place may not be appropriate for another.

> *How to get connected to and develop work with the Internet*
>
> If you are interested in connecting to the Internet, then follow these simple steps:
>
> 1. Find out where your school is connected. Talk to your head teacher about access and why geography (and history) will benefit from this technology.
> 2. Find out where you are able to get free access, perhaps via a higher education institution, for your first experience.
> 3. Buy *The Guardian* every Thursday and monitor the *Online* supplement for ideas.
> 4. Buy one of the monthly Internet magazines from the newsagents.
> 5. There is no need to attend expensive conferences of technological experts. You may even find that some of your students know enough to get you started – especially if they have access to the Internet at home. In such cases, there is a danger that the students may become frustrated by your relative lack of know-how, so the quicker you learn and catch up, the better.
> 6. Try out the BBC Education On-line (Figure 9) for your first experience of the Internet. They try to ensure that it is jargon-free and offers some support and interpretation. In addition, useful research material used to create geography programmes will be available.
> 7. Look at UK educational sites – for example: BECTa research and development website (www.becta.org.uk/).
>
> and later …
>
> 8. Do some searching yourself, then send an e-mail to chris.durbin@staffordshire.gov.uk about what you have found and how you have used it.
> 9. Find a few partner schools in other places to share geographic teaching ideas by e-mail.
> 10. With your IT co-ordinator, investigate with your Internet access provider how to create pages for your own school. Under a section on the local environment, create pages about a local issue of interest to others studying geography.

Conclusion

The Internet is another resource to add to the geography teacher's repertoire. Its unique property is that it positively encourages communication between users through interaction, feedback and the exchange of ideas – all of which can be achieved easily and quickly and at a global scale. It can be frustrating and infuriating to use at first, but you will soon grow in confidence and communicate with others (including your students) who can help to find solutions. However, do not cast out the textbooks in the stock cupboard just yet! Use the Internet to enable your geography lessons to be investigative, up-to-the-minute, relevant and exciting. The result will be that your students will see the relevance of their geographical education and will become globally and culturally more aware. Many of them, because they can use the Internet at home, may already be more aware than you are – a fact that can be turned to advantage in the classroom. ■

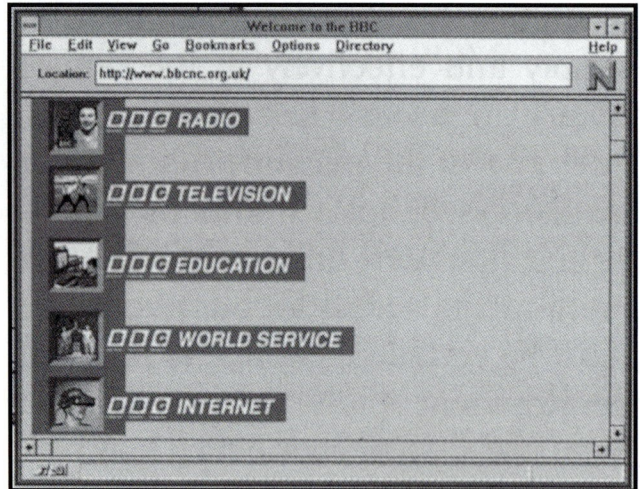

Figure 9: The BBC Education homepage http://www.bbc.co.uk/education

Editor's notes

1. The original Kobe earthquake site featured in this article is no longer available on the World Wide Web, however, some useful websites and information can be found by simply typing 'Kobe' into a search engine. Three such sites are:
   - www.std.kobe-u.ac.jp/newsnet/Eng/quake
   - www.eqc.com/publications/Kobe
   - www.city.Kobe.jp/cityoffice/15/020/quake
2. The BBC (www.bbc.co.uk/education-webguide/pkg_main.p_home) provides a good starting-point for educational websites. It includes short reviews (written by subject specialists) on each website.

Acknowledgements

Len Brown for his love of geography on television. Julie Wright for introducing us to the joys of the Internet. BBC Education Officer colleagues for their positive encouragement.

> *Chris Durbin was Education Officer at BBC Education, London, and is now Inspector for Geography, Staffordshire LEA. He is now engaged in developing a website for geography teachers in Staffordshire (www.sln.org.uk/geography). There are many useful links for all geography teachers across the UK. Roger Sanders teaches at Sir John Talbot School, Whitchurch, Shropshire (e-mail: sirjohnta.syss@bbcnc.org.uk).*

Software and hardware

10 Making the most of images

David Hassell and members of the GA's **Information Technology Working Group** investigate digital cameras

The old adage 'a picture is worth a thousand words' is a concept geography teachers always try to make the most of in their lessons. However, prints or slides have a number of limitations when used in the geography classroom, which the use of digital cameras can overcome. The concept of linking a camera to a computer is not new but, until recently (1998), it was an expensive and complicated process. Today's digital cameras provide a wealth of opportunities for the teacher and the student.

The pros and cons of using digital cameras

Digital cameras are as simple to use in the field as traditional film cameras. Digital cameras with small liquid crystal display (LCD) screens allow the photographer to view their handiwork and, if they are not happy with the image, have another try. As many digital cameras come with extra memory space it is possible to take lots of pictures. Perhaps the two most important advantages over traditional cameras are:

1. there are no ongoing film and processing costs, and
2. the pictures can be accessed at any time (you do not have to wait until the film is finished).

Some digital cameras drain their batteries quite quickly, although using rechargeable batteries will save you money. Once taken, pictures can be downloaded onto a computer or displayed on a television screen. Pictures that have been downloaded can then be wiped from the camera memory, leaving it clear for re-use.

The biggest advantages for schools is that after downloading images to a computer, you can load them straight into a word processed document, use them in a multimedia presentation or place them onto the school website. You can adapt and enhance pictures which, despite your best efforts, still do not show all you intended. Using picture editing software you can 'clean up' the image, cut out and/or enlarge a specific section, add labels, draw in a new road or building ... the list is endless.

Digital cameras and geography

Fieldwork offers the best use of digital cameras: students can use digital images to illustrate their fieldwork investigation. Pictures can be used either as they were taken or with explanatory labels added; they can be edited to show changes in the environment (e.g. before and after a specific event) or, where only small sections are required, pictures can be electronically cut up. Students fieldwork or enquiry results can be produced on desk-top publishing, multimedia or website authoring packages with the digital images imported into the text.

The quality of many inexpensive colour printers means that images from a digital camera can be used by geography teachers to produce task/resource sheets. Alternatively, to reduce the cost of printing, images can be utilised electronically. The whole class can view images from a digital camera on a television screen or overhead projector. A presentation (see Rogers, 1998), multimedia or word-processing package offers you the opportunity to combine digital images and other information for your geography lessons and present them on the school network, to students working in groups or individually.

Students increasingly use software packages for completing a piece of writing and a supply of suitable pictures can offer effective support for differentiation. Students can use images from a digital camera, either as exemplification or to help them with their writing, with the direction of the teacher.

The variety of digital cameras

Digital video cameras remain beyond the budget of many schools (good ones cost more than £1500 and the highest

One of the originals from which the 1024 x 768 image was taken.

The difference in quality between two resolutions – 1024 x 768 on the left and 640 x 480 on the right. The original image was only 2cm high.

quality still cameras are expensive), nevertheless you and your colleagues may be able to make a case for purchasing a digital still camera for cross-curricular use. The way in which digital cameras work is more or less standard. Different models, however, provide different facilities and methods for transferring the images to a computer. Most cameras include autofocus, a flash, a user manual, leads (for connection to computer/television), computer software and a power adapter (sometimes priced separately).

Planning your picture

Most digital cameras have a normal viewfinder and a few have a single lens reflex one. A growing number include an LCD which allows you to see the picture before you take it and review your handiwork afterwards. Be warned, however, LCD facilities quickly use up battery power.

Camera features

The number of functions increases each time a new model of digital camera is introduced. These include taking multiple shots, a timer, a date stamp, a macro mode for close-ups and integral rechargeable batteries. More advanced facilities include 5-6 seconds of multiple shots to illustrate action index prints, software for printing in various modes with a dedicated printer and the production of panoramic images. Specialised software is also available which allows you to link together a number of images to produce virtual reality 360° panoramas (Howarth, 1998).

Picture quality or resolution

Pictures are captured using a collection of light sensitive pixels, the number determining the quality of the picture. Less expensive digital cameras have 640 x 480 pixels – the same as many computer screens – some have even less. An increasing number of cameras offer more than one resolution, which allows you to choose the quality of image before you take it. Basically the higher the resolution the bigger the memory space required to save it, however, the higher the resolution the more a picture can be enlarged and the better the quality (see photographs opposite).

Camera memory

Most digitial cameras come with 2 or 4mb of memory as standard (with the option to enlarge their storage capacity). Some use a fixed internal memory, while others have removable 'Flash' memory cards: which can be replaced with larger ones. A few digital cameras include memory cards which can be plugged directly into a suitable computer. One of the latest models has a mini disk which can hold 670mb of pictures – that should keep you and your students busy!

Camera-to-computer connection

There are four basic methods of connecting a digital camera to a computer, the most common of which is a lead from the camera to the computer. Cameras with flash memory cards have an adapter into which the cards fit, this can be inserted into a floppy disk drive. For others a device called Camera Connect links to the computer and accepts memory cards. Both these approaches allow the memory to be accessed quickly. Some cards also have PCMCIA memory which can be plugged into a slot on a portable computer and accessed like a hard disk. One final approach is the infra-red link; here the camera-computer link must be compatible.

Picture format

Many digital cameras have their own internal format for images. You simply load the software provided with the camera (see below) onto a computer. Pictures downloaded from such cameras to the computer can then be saved in their own specific format or other formats, e.g. *JPEG*, *GIF* and *BMP*. Other cameras can be plugged straight into the computer and pictures can be saved in a common format, e.g. *JPEG*.

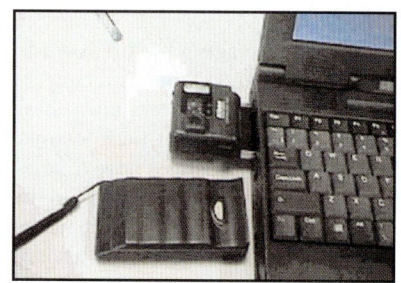

The Coolpix 100 snaps into two parts the main section of which is a PCMCIA card which can be plugged directly into a portable computer.

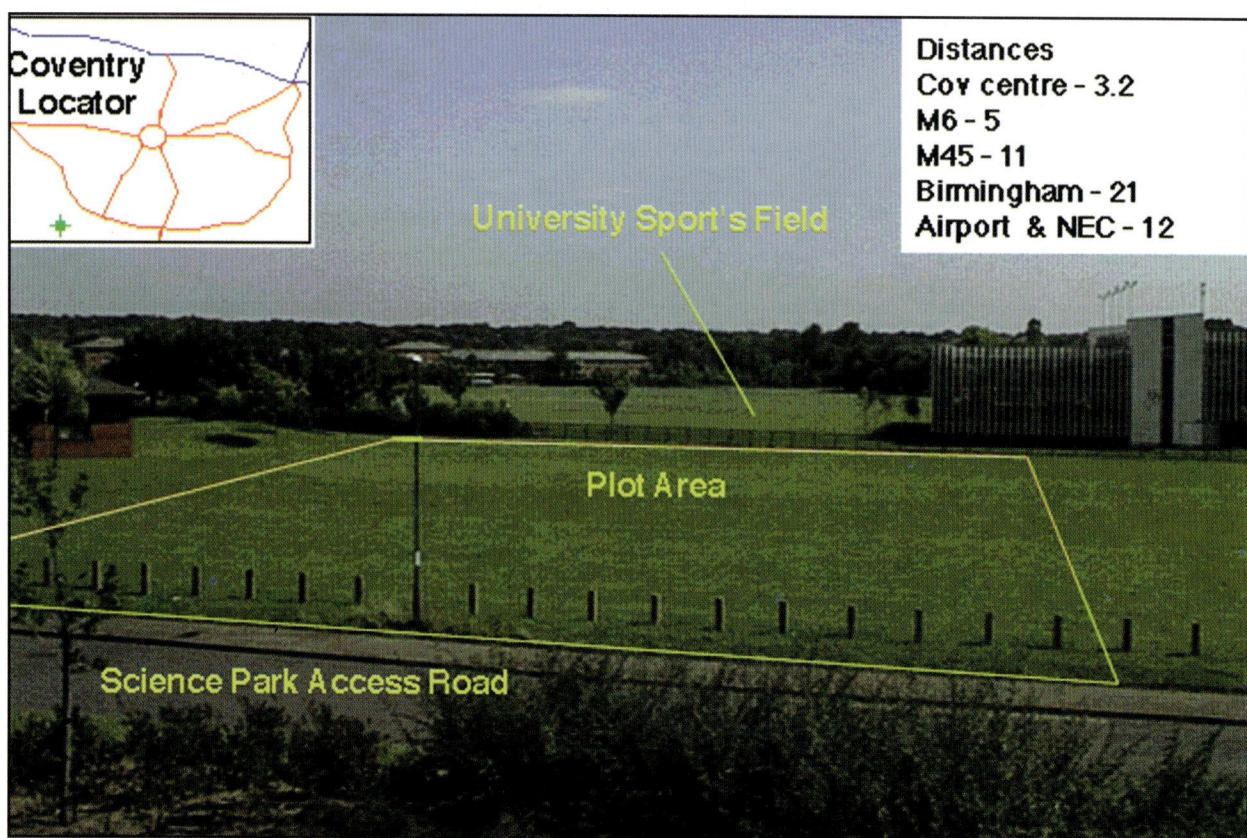

One image from an enquiry into best location for a service company.

Software

Virtually all digital cameras come with a serial link and some include software. This software allows you to download the pictures from the camera and control it, for example, to delete stored images and take photographs via the computer.

A few cameras come with more advanced image manipulation software or this can be purchased separately. This software provides a wide range of facilities ranging from those really intended for the professional (and priced accordingly) to those which will meet the needs of most geography teachers and students. For instance, they allow you to cut, crop and change the brightness and colour in your picture.

Examples of the cameras available

The increase in the number of digital cameras available has meant a continuing reduction in price, an improvement in resolution and more functions. We looked at the facilities offered by four cameras within the £200-£350 price band. These represent a sample and are not recommendations to purchase (to obtain further information contact the producers and suppliers or look at their websites).

- Casio qv700, resolution 640x480, storage 2mb compactflash with 47 economy, 26 normal or 14 high quality images, LCD viewfinder, serial connection and software. Price: £230.
- CoolPix 100, resolution 512x480, storage 1mb PCMCIA internal memory with 42 normal and 21 fine quality images in JPEG format, LCD viewfinder. Price: £45.
- Kodak DC200, resolution up to 1152 x 864, storage compact flash with 4mb (13 high and 60 low quality images), LCD monitor and viewfinder, zoom, serial and video connection plus software. Price: £199.
- Fuji DX-10 Digital Camera Zoom, resolution up to 1024 x 768, storage compact flash with 2mb Smart Media (6 high and 13 low quality images), LCD monitor and viewfinder, zoom, serial and video connection plus software. Price: £169.

Choosing a camera

Computer magazines often have tests of a number of cameras and the website addresses listed below offer further information. The questions below may be useful in helping you make a decision on which model to purchase:

A site ripe for redevelopment, taking images such as this can form part of a whole class fieldwork exercise.

- How do you envisage using the camera?
- How important is the resolution of the image? What is the minimum you would accept?
- Do you want to take close-up shots?
- Does your computer have a PCMCIA slot for simple downloading?
- Would you use the television link?
- How many pictures would you take before you return to the computer?
- Is ease of downloading an issue?
- What software is included?

To get a feel for digital cameras borrow a friend or colleague's camera, take pictures, download and access them on your computer. Our only advice is: buy the best quality you can afford and do not be seduced by 'wizzy' features. ■

Author's note

Since this article was written the cost of basic digital cameras has come down. The range of features and the resolution continue to increase along with the amount of memory. In addition, more cameras now come with removable memory. Students can transfer images from cameras to the computer and insert them into, for example, a multimedia presentation or a word-processed document, as part of their coursework. Teachers are now putting images taken during fieldwork onto their intranet, for use as a student resource, or the school website to illustrate school activities.

Editor's note

Digital images can be used in presentation software such as *PowerPoint*. Students can devise material for a slide show and view it on a computer screen before producing the slides (pages 30-31), or a teacher can present a high-tech slide show (pages 32-33).

Contact/website

Actiontec (Camera Connect) – Tel: 01782 753355
Adobe – Tel: 0181 606 4001
Agfa – Tel: 0181 231 4200; website: http://www.agfahome.com/ephoto/home.html
Canon – Tel: 0121 680 8062; website: http://www.cannon.co.uk/
Casio – Tel: 0181 450 9131; website: http://www.casio.com/html/products/cproducts.html
Epson – Tel: 01442 261144; website: http://www.epson.co.uk
Fujifilm – Tel: 0171 586 5900; website: http://www.fujifilm.com/home/sbu/electimg/ei_consu.htm
Hewlett Packard – Tel: 0118 969 6622; website: http://www.photosmart.com/products/products.html
JVC – Tel: 0181 207 7654; website: http://www.jvc<<europe.com/all2.m4?sc=enen
Kodak – Tel: 0800 281487; website: http://www.kodak.com/cgi®bin/webCatalog.pl?category=Digital+Cameras
MicroGrafx – Tel: 01483 747526
MetaCreations – Tel: 01756 704000
Nikon – Tel: 0181 541 4440; website: http://www.nikon.co.uk/eid/index.htm
Olympus – Tel: 0800 072 0070; website: http://www.olympusamerica.com/digital/docs/digproduct.html
Panasonic – 0990 357357; website: http://www.panasonic.co.uk/
Ricoh – Tel: 0178275355; website: http://www.ricoh®cameras.co.uk/digital/index.html
Sanyo – Tel: 01923 477302; website: http://www.sanyo.co.uk/
Sony – 01635 869500; website: http://www.sony.com/
Vivitar – Tel: 01793 544829 website: http://www.vivitar.co.uk/digital/index.html

Reference

Howarth, M. (1998) 'Virtual reality photography: a new tool for primary geographers', *Primary Geography*, 33, pp. 28-9.
Rogers, S. (1998) 'Presentation software', *Teaching Geography*, 23, 3, pp. 150-1.

David Hassell is Chair of the GA IT Working Group and Head of Curriculum and Institutional Development at the British Educational Communications and Technology Agency.
e-mail: david_hassell@becta.org.uk

Software and hardware

11 Presentation software

Steve Rogers investigates the potential of presentation software for geography teachers (1998)

Introduction

At a recent geography conference the overhead projector looked decidedly redundant in the corner of the stage, as speaker after speaker made their presentations with the aid of a presentation software package. Instead of the usual collection of overhead transparencies, each speaker inserted their disks into the computer and proceeded to present their lectures electronically, making use of 'flying' text, graphics and, in some cases, sound effects and video. They had clearly moved on to the exciting new opportunities provided by such packages. The final speaker manoeuvred the overhead projector centre stage for a more traditional presentation. Yet those transparencies looked very familiar - they had been produced on *PowerPoint*.

What is a presentation package?

Microsoft *PowerPoint* is one of a number of presentation packages which normally come as part of the suite of office software often provided with new machines or networks. *PowerPoint* comes as part of *Microsoft Office*, and *Lotus Office*, *WordPerfect* and *Claris Works* packages offer similar functionality.

The packages are easy to use and an increasing number of useful guides are available. *PowerPoint* can be used to create an electronic slide-show presentation, supplements (such as handouts), and speaker's notes. Slides may include a mixture of text, graphics, clip art, tables, maps, drawings, animation, video clips, visual materials created in and imported from other applications, and sound. The images produced can be printed to create overhead transparencies and 35mm slides or a 'slide show' can be run on the computer screen. Presentation packages offer a range of visual effects for your slide show: for example, text and graphics can be made to move around or fade in and out on-screen. One of the most powerful aspects of presentation software is that it allows you to manipulate text and images into an effective display. You can easily edit or (using templates provided) format text, and add emphases or levels of importance to particular items.

Linked to appropriate equipment, a slide show can be projected onto a large flat screen (either through an overhead projector computer display panel or directly). Although neither system is cheap, recent reductions in price mean that more schools are purchasing them. Increasingly, computers can also output the image in a format for display on a large television screen.

This software offers exciting possibilities for geography teachers and students alike. First, it allows students to

Figure 1: Three slides prepared by year 8 students for use in a presentation. The climate graphs were produced in the spreadsheet package *Excel* and pasted onto the slides.

ITALY - DIFFERENCES IN CLIMATE

- Milan is much wetter with rainfall throughout the year.
- Palermo is drier with a summer drought. This is typical of a Meditteranean Climate.
- Milan has colder winters and a more extreme climate. The range of temperature is 23°C.
- Palermo is warmer in winter and hot in summer. The temperature range is 15°C.

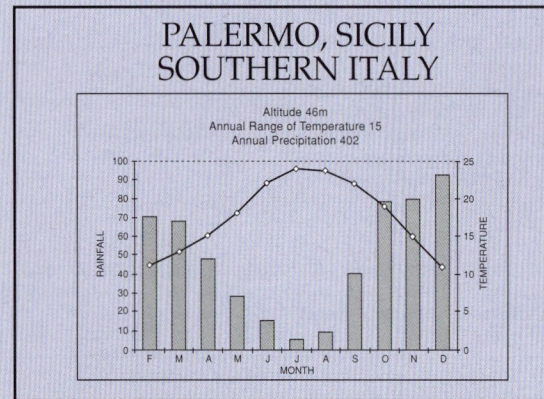

PALERMO, SICILY
SOUTHERN ITALY

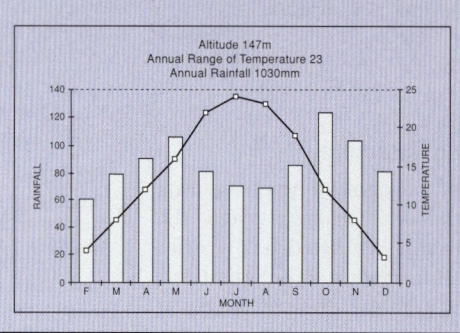

MILAN - NORTHERN ITALY

develop their IT skills. By using the software, they also focus on literacy skills such as communicating information to a specific audience, for example, when making presentations to other students. Second, geography teachers will increasingly have the opportunity to use it as a teaching resource. The examples below indicate how presentation software can be used in the geography classroom. Beyond the classroom, the software has potential for supporting presentations to parents, governors and colleagues.

Using presentation packages in the geography classroom

Italy's North-South divide

Towards the end of a four-week unit on Italy, year 8 students were encouraged to present a summary of what they had learnt in the form of a slide show. Working in pairs, using *PowerPoint*, students were required to describe and explain their findings on the different physical, social and economic factors between the north and the south of Italy. We also planned to use this as a consolidation and assessment exercise. Students were briefly shown how to produce visual effects and paste images onto the slides. Earlier in the unit, students had produced climate graphs (for Palermo and Milan) using a spreadsheet. They were encouraged to incorporate these graphs into their presentation, together with a textual analysis of the differences (Figure 1). A flat-bed scanner was available, so some students decided to scan photographs from books for inclusion in their presentations. Students then presented their slide show to the whole class. The teacher selected some slides for printing in colour to use as part of a classroom display. The students produced handouts of their slides which were assessed by the teacher.

Assessing the environmental impact of a wind farm

After a year 10 field visit to a wind farm, one half of a group of GCSE students was asked to make the case for a new wind farm in mid-Wales and the other was asked to oppose the development. Students were given the opportunity to produce a leaflet using a text package or to make their case with an electronic presentation. Most of the students were unfamiliar with the presentation software and so started to word-process their leaflets. However, once their peers demonstrated the use of interesting backgrounds, 'flying' text and animated graphics, they all switched to the presentation package and experimented with the effects. Students located the British Wind Energy website on the Internet and set about electronically cutting and pasting images and maps onto their slides. During their field visit, students had photographed the wind farm using an ion camera (this records images of particle movement around the blades of the turbines) and these images were incorporated into one presentation.

Beyond the classroom: presenting information at a parents' evening

One head of geography prepared an electronic presentation to show to parents of prospective students at the annual open evening. Using the presentation software, she created ten slides which informed parents about the content of the key stage 3 course and gave a summary of the approaches used. The page describing the field study programme offered in year 7 is shown in Figure 2.

Conclusion

Presentation software provides geography teachers with a dynamic way of displaying information. Its greatest potential is realised when students of geography have the opportunity to present their ideas to a specific audience using such packages. Presentation packages such as *PowerPoint* enable students to generate and organise ideas, and allow them to develop their communication skills further. The increasing availability of presentation packages on school computer networks and at home is already making an impact. If schools are to follow the trend in the business world, it will not be long before *PowerPoint* is a common feature of the geography classroom. ■

Fieldwork in Year 7

◆ Three days at the LEAs field study centre in June (optional)

◆ Local fieldwork in each term:

◆ Term 1 – farm study

◆ Term 2 – river study

◆ Term 3 – village study

Figure 2: An example of a slide produced in *PowerPoint* showing a synopsis of one school's year 7 fieldwork programme.

Editor's note

Scanners and digital cameras can be used to input geographical images into presentation packages, such as *PowerPoint*. The images can then be labelled or manipulated to highlight key aspects (pages 27-29) and displayed using an electronic projector, electronic board or LCD display (pages 32-33).

Further information

User guides to *PowerPoint* include:

PowerPoint Made Simple by Moira Stephen (Made Simple Books, price £8.99). An easy-to-follow jargon-free guide, ideal for the beginner.

Microsoft PowerPoint At A Glance by Microsoft Press (price £15.49). A well-illustrated comprehensive guide which takes the user through from the basics to a higher order use of the software.

Steve Rogers is County Adviser for Geography and Environmental Education in Shropshire and is a member of the GA's Information Technology Working Group.

Software and hardware

12 Whole-class computer activities

Do you have only one computer available? **David Hassell** *outlines ways in which it can be used for whole-class teaching (1999)*

Most schools have a large display screen on which material can be projected for whole-class viewing. Using a computer in conjunction with this screen opens up a range of opportunities for stimulating students, illustrating difficult concepts or simply collating and co-ordinating information and ideas. This approach is ideal for whole-class teaching and is also suitable for students to present their findings.

Teacher presentations

Many geography teachers use presentation packages, e.g. *Powerpoint*, in the classroom. However, some feel its use can lead to overhead transparencies simply being replaced by computers. However, as Rogers (1998) explained, the use of presentation packages offers advantages for the geography classroom, teachers can, for example:

- mix pictures, video and text in a format that is simple to use and which conveys information in a more powerful way than traditional methods,
- adapt material for mixed ability groups without having to start from scratch, and
- change things on the display just before or even during the lesson.

In addition, presentation material can be stored in a flexible format for colleagues who can then adapt it for their own use.

Internet and digital images

The Internet and the use of digital cameras (Hassell, 1998) both offer opportunities to obtain stimulating images and information for exciting geography lessons. Teachers can use digital cameras to prepare a selection of images for a particular purpose. For example, images of potential sites for a superstore can be projected onto a large screen to stimulate a whole-class discussion on locational issues. Images stored from previous years can extend discussion on fieldwork activities, or be combined with other more complex resources and displayed on screen for more effective teaching.

Spreadsheet or other modelling packages provide opportunities for teachers to encourage students to pose 'What if ...?' questions. Teachers can display models of difficult or abstract geographical concepts on spreadsheets and project them onto a large screen to inform a whole-class discussion. Students' suggestions on amendments or revisions to the spreadsheet can be incorporated immediately.

Many CD-ROMS include high quality animations and interactive elements which provide an effective explanation of a geographical process. Where a CD-ROM package has been designed for student use, but it is impractical to book the school IT suite or arrange individual access. It can be displayed on a large screen and discussed with the whole-class. This approach can be used to demonstrate proper use of complex software packages to students.

Collating and examining evidence

A large screen can be used to collate class fieldwork or investigation data. This provides an opportunity to discuss specific points as they arise. Spreadsheets can be set up in advance with statistics that calculate or graphs that draw automatically when data is added. There are a number of advantages to using this approach:

- data can be input and/or updated and mistakes rectified quickly,
- the format of the spreadsheet can be revised as necessary,
- complex data can be displayed and analysed during whole-class discussion.

Student presentations

Presentation software enables students to use and display images, text and other resources from a wide range of sources and is a powerful medium for them to communicate their ideas. To encourage students to concentrate on key elements of their argument provide them with a presentation template together with information on the maximum number of slides and a word or time limit. Less able students will benefit from additional support in the form of an outline structure for the presentation.

What equipment do I need?

Essentially the equipment required depends on the mode of projection and the specification of the computer that you are planning to use. As there are a number of options available you are advised to discuss the compatibility of existing hardware with your IT co-ordinator and potential suppliers. Each option is dealt with separately below.

A television

This is the simplest and least expensive option for getting started. The disadvantages are that televisions often have low resolution screens and not all computers can be connected to them. Some computers have an integral television board so all you need to purchase is a connecting cable, and boards which can be fitted to most PC/PC-compatible or Macintosh computers cost from £45. For other desktops VGA/XGA-television adapters can be purchased from £125, and for laptops PCMCIA-television adapters cost from £225.

Large screen monitor

These are expensive to buy. However, the greatest advantage is that they can be used to display video, television and

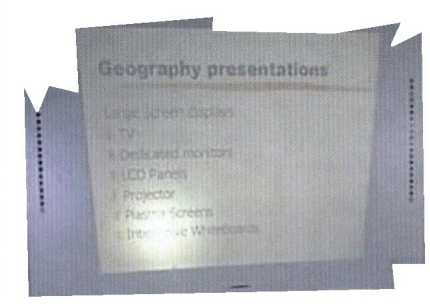

Figure 1: **LCD screen in use on an overhead projector.** *Photo:* **David Hassell.**

data input. Prices range from just over £1000 for a 29inch screen to over £2500.

LCD panels

Liquid crystal display panels can be connected to a computer, laid on an overhead projector and the image projected onto a screen (Figure 1). Some laptops have a detachable screen which can double as an LCD panel. Although mobile LCDs require a good quality overhead projector (OHP) (minimum 400W) and the type of OHP found in most schools is not of acceptable quality. In addition the image is not very visible in bright light. Prices range from £850 to £1400.

Electronic projectors

Electronic projectors can be connected directly to computers and used to project the image onto a screen. They vary in price from £1200 to over £8000 and the price tends to reflect the quality of resolution, brightness and weight of the equipment. The brighter the projector, the better the image and the higher the light conditions in which it can be used. Most electronic projectors are very portable and will accept video and data input.

Plasma displays

Plasma displays or screens are large flat monitors (4-6 inches thick and from 32 x 50 inches in size) and, as this is relatively new technology, are expensive to purchase (£4000+). However, prices are being reduced constantly and plasma displays now provide a viable option to large televisions. Like electronic projectors they accept both data and video input, the added advantage is that plasma screens can be used any light conditions.

Interactive boards

These are sometimes called 'Smart' boards, but the name is not helpful as interactive boards require three pieces of equipment: a computer, a projector and a touch-sensitive whiteboard (the latter two are sold as a package). You connect your computer to the projector and the interactive board and the on-screen image is projected onto the board. You control the computer by pointing at active elements on the interactive board using either your finger or an electronic 'pen'.

Interactive boards have the same advantages and disadvantages of electronic projectors in terms of quality of images, and have added features and a greater range of use. The packages (projector and board) start at £6000.

Which solution is right for you?

'Cheap and cheerful' options (television connected to computer) produce low-quality displays that are suitable for use where resolution is not an issue. More expensive and better quality options include interactive boards. Each option has advantages and disadvantages – some of which have been described above. The key issue is the specific compatibility of existing hardware and it is vital to discuss this with your IT co-ordinator and supplier. Ask yourself:

1. How do I envisage using the large screen display?
- to present images
- for word processing
- for collating data, e.g. spreadsheets/data-handling
- to access multimedia, e.g. CD-ROM or the Internet
- for use with other types of software

The lower resolution of television screens does not allow for a readable display of smaller text and details, for example from Internet pages.

2. Where do I anticipate using the equipment?
- in one or several classrooms
- in an IT suite
- throughout the school

Some equipment is more portable than others; some interactive boards must be wall or ceiling mounted; and low light level projectors, for instance, will need to be used in a room which has blackout facilities.

3. To what computer(s) do I anticipate connecting the display device?
- Macintosh desk/laptop
- Acorn desk/laptop
- PC desk/laptop

Not all equipment can be used with each type of computer. Consider the age and/or specification of computers before purchasing equipment. Consider also:

- Future purchases for compatibility, e.g. do you have the correct connectors or are extra adapters and/or cables needed?
- Whether the software will run on your computer, e.g. for interactive boards?
- The screen resolution output from your computer, e.g. VGA, SVGA, XGA?

The information on equipment in this article is based on work completed by the British Educational Communications and Technology Agency (BECTa); up-to-date details can be found on the BECTa website in the IT guidance section (see below). BECTa is investigating the pedagogy of whole-class computer technologies and will provide further information on its website during 2000.

If you use large screen technology in your geography classroom and would be willing to share your experiences through *Teaching Geography* please contact David Hassell via GA headquarters or e-mail david_hassell@becta.org.uk

Internet sources and suppliers

Reviews and information on some of the products described in this article is available at: *Personal Computer World* - www.pcw.co.uk/ *PC Direct* - www.pcdirect.co.uk/ and *Zdnet* - www.zdnet.co.uk/pcmag/labs/1999/04/data_projectors/

Computer to television adapters/cables: Betterbox (01908 560200, www.betterbox.com/), Fox Direct (0990 744500, www.foxdirect.co.uk/), Hills Components (01923 424344), Insight (0800 706 0510, www.insight.com/), Misco (01933 400400, www.misco.co.uk/)

Interactive whiteboards: Accurate, Matrix (0800 980 9864, www.matrixdisplay.com/), Promethean (01254 676921, www.promethean.co.uk/), Vupoint (01438 716564, www.vupoint.co.uk/)

LCD panels: Misco, Pico Direct (0870 729 6097, www.picodirect.co.uk/), Presentation Direct (0800 174164), Presentations by Design (020 8450 3488)

Large screen monitors: Atomwide (01689 814500, www.atomwide.co.uk/)

Projectors: Accurate (0113 250 0500, www.accurate.plc.uk/), Atomwide, Boxlight (01732 840404, www.boxlight.com/), Just Projectors (07000 587877, www.projectors.co.uk/), Matrix, Pico Direct, Presentation Direct, Tech direct (020 8286 2222, www.techdirect.co.uk/), Vupoint, W2.FM Direct (0118 973 0855, www.w2fm.co.uk/)

Plasma displays: Tech direct, W2.FM Direct.

Up-to-date details on equipment can be found on the BECTa website under 'Information' in the IT guidance section at: www.becta.org.uk/info-sheets/display.html

References

Rogers, S. (1998) 'Presentation software', *Teaching Geography*, 23, 3, pp. 150-1.
Hassell, D. (1998) 'Making the most of images', *Teaching Geography*, 23, 4, pp. 206-8

David Hassell is the Chair of the Information Technology Working Group of the GA and works at BECTa in the schools directorate. E-mail: david_hassell@becta.org.uk

Software and hardware

13 Satellite images and IT capability

Michael Barnett and **Mike Milton** explore land-use with colour displays

The European Space Agency has just (1995) launched another earth observation satellite (ERS-2) which will provide 105 million pieces of information about the earth each second. This satellite sends radar waves to earth and measures their reflection, providing a wealth of useful information for geographers. However, the main types of satellites providing images which can be used in teaching are weather satellites, such as METEOSAT, and land observation satellites, such as the American Landsat and the French SPOT. The SPOT satellite collects 27 million pieces of information for each 60 by 60km square that it passes over.

Figure 1: Very near infra-red image of East Kent shown in shades of grey.
(Data supplied courtesy of NRSC)

Sense can only be made of the enormous amount of data by using computers. For example, computers enable schools to obtain, store and display both weather and land observation satellite images. Data from the land observation satellites is available for schools from an increasing number of sources. Some schools and colleges already have software (e.g. TeraVue, Multi Spectral View II, PDSView and Dartcom's Weather Capture System) which will process this data so that students can create their own remotely-sensed images. Affordable data is also available on CD-ROMs (e.g. Satellite Explorer 1 and 2).

Most schools now have satellite images in the form of posters, textbook illustrations or specially produced packs, but students often make little use of them as learning resources for their own enquiries. Now that the unmanageable demands of the original National Curriculum have been reduced, the time is right for geography departments to review their key stage 3 teaching and seek to develop and widen students' enquiries to encompass a range of resources, including satellite images.

For schools with little experience of using satellite images, the first step is likely to be the use of *products* of information technology in the form of a paper copy of an image. This is an important *application of information technology*, especially as an increasing number of our students will use satellite images as part of their jobs. A key purpose of the Geographical Association's publication *Images of Earth: A teacher's guide to remote sensing in geography at key stage 3 and GCSE* (Barnett *et al.*, 1995) was to provide teachers with the basic knowledge and understanding of satellites and computer processing to interpret these images and their unusual use of colour.

The revised Orders for Information Technology place increased emphasis on the use of computers to aid students in their own geographical investigations. The number of computers in schools is increasing and students' own IT capability is benefiting from improved provision in both primary and secondary schools. Some geography departments have already taught students to use image-processing software to investigate a sequence of weather images or to create their own earth observation images using data provided on a floppy disk. For example, one GCSE class used a sequence of images showing the passage of a depression with data from a weather station and newspapers. At another school, students investigated local green space using a SPOT image based on infra-red light which vegetation strongly reflects.

The benefit of image processing is that students can create images that provide the information most relevant to their own particular investigations. This will be a future development for many geography departments, but all should be aware of the potential value of image processing to students' understanding of geography, as well as their IT capability. *Images of Earth* includes an introduction to satellite-image processing, which intends to be comprehensible to the non-specialist, together with data on floppy disks for producing images of St Lucia, London Docklands and East Kent.

The Landsat satellite has a thematic mapper sensor that records six types or bands of light and one band of radiant heat. The sequence of images of East Kent shows how different colours can be used for the same area to emphasise different land-use information. Figure 1 shows an image based on band 4 (very near infra-red light) which vegetation reflects strongly. Consequently, thriving vegetation is bright (e.g. along the meandering Stour valley) while bare fields and the urban areas of the coastal towns are dark.

Figure 2 combines three bands of light. The satellite recorded blue, green and red light and these are displayed in blue, red and green respectively just as they are in a colour television. This combined image is called a true-colour composite but is rather dull, mainly because of the effects of haze but also because vegetation absorbs much visible light for photosynthesis and so has a relatively low reflectance.

Two visible bands of light and one very near infra-red band have been combined to create the image in Figure 3. The brightest band is the infra-red which vegetation reflects strongly. This controls the red gun in the colour display, and so vegetation is shown as red.

One visible band of light (red) and two infra-red bands have been used to create Figure 4. The red light controls the blue gun in the colour display and the two different infra-reds control the green and red guns. Because two infra-red bands have been used, the image distinguishes between different types of vegetation. For example, deep oranges and reds show the water meadows of the Stour valley, while greenish yellows show urban parks and, most notably, the fairways of golf courses on the North Foreland and near Sandwich.

Figure 5 is created from the same bands of light as Figure 4, but they are shown by different colours. The red

Figure 2: **Natural colour image.**
(Data supplied courtesy of NRSC)

Figure 3: **Vegetation is image.**
(Data supplied courtesy of NRSC)

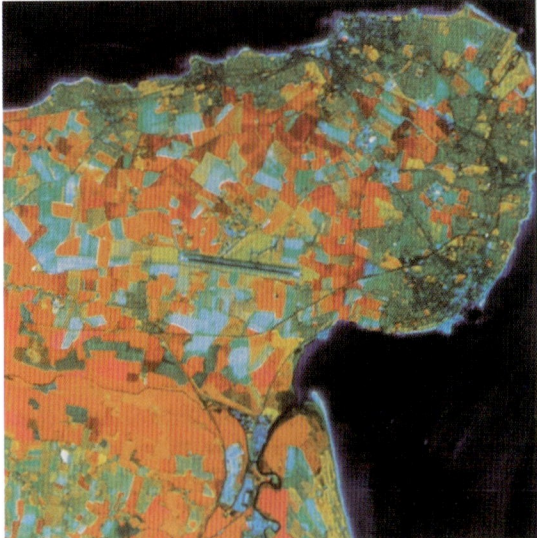

Figure 4: **Vegetation is yellow/orange image.**
(Data supplied courtesy of NRSC)

Figure 5: **Vegetation is green image.**
(Data supplied courtesy of NRSC)

light controls the blue gun in the colour display and the two infra-reds still control the green and red but have been switched round. This shows vegetation as different shades of green, but bare fields are shown as pink. The colour arrangement in Figure 4 is often preferred to this, as the eye does not so readily distinguish between slightly differing shades of green as it does between slightly differing shades of other colours.

These different images of East Kent have been created using the same set of data from Landsat and provided on a floppy disk. The image processing software has allowed different images to be created to show different features of the area's geography. The images provide examples of the three conventions used in remote sensing to show vegetation in satellite images: green, red and orange.

These images of East Kent are valuable resources for studying land-use, whether it is studied as part of whole-class teaching or individual enquiries at GCSE or A-level. Satellite images provide up-to-date information, and the false colours help to differentiate between different land-uses. In addition, these images cover large areas and make it possible to identify patterns over a wider area. Collection of land-use data by fieldwork is very time-consuming, but the image may provide a context for an enquiry within a smaller area. Linking fieldwork to an image helps to interpret more accurately the different types of vegetation shown by different shades of a colour. Consequently, broader patterns of land-use can be identified in more detail. This is just one example of how satellite images can be used in the classroom, and there are many others in *Images of Earth*. ■

Acknowledgement

NRSC Ltd for permission to use the Landsat data which was processed to create the images of East Kent by the Remote Sensing in Geography Project at the University of London Institute of Education.

Reference and further information

Barnett, M., Kent, A. and Milton, M. (eds) (1995) *Images of Earth: A teacher's guide to remote sensing in geography at key stage 3 and GCSE*. Sheffield: Geographical Association (out of print).

The *Images of Earth* publication is no longer available, but there are several useful websites which have satellite images that can be downloaded. Try:

http://www.nottingham.co.uk/meteosat for meteosat images.

http://www.usgs.gov/Earthshots for images taken on different dates.

Michael Barnett is a Professor at Imperial College, London and works within the Applied Optics Group and Mike Milton is based at the University of London, Institute of Education.

Software and hardware

14 A guide to geographic information systems

Diana Freeman, David Green and **David Hassell** offer a guide to new GIS software and digitised data (1994)

What is a computer GIS?

A geographical information system (GIS) has the ability to store, retrieve, manipulate and analyse a wide range of spatially-related data in order to produce maps. With a GIS the user may ask questions of the data related to the map, search for patterns and distributions and investigate the underlying relationships between different sets of data. A computer-based GIS handles data quickly and efficiently, providing mapping facilities that would take a person many hours or even days to complete by hand. A GIS also leads to the creation of new data.

The scope and facilities of computer-based GIS vary considerably. In its simplest form a GIS has database facilities and can display data on a map according to a query on the database. At the top end of the range are complex packages used by planning departments, oil companies or environmental agencies, which provide advanced relational databases and mapping facilities. These can cope with different types of data and maps according to the type of information that needs to be processed and the form of the map output required.

Raster and Vector GIS

These two main types of GIS have different methods of displaying and using maps and data associated with the maps.

Raster GIS

A raster is a grid of cells overlaid on a map or picture. On computer this is a matrix of screen pixels (picture elements). The location of each cell is identified and has a value added to it. The value may be a numerical code, for instance, the cell, R3, C2 in Figure 1 could have code 1 which represents conifers on a map of vegetation types. A raster map may have several layers of data such as vegetation, soils or geology that may either be viewed separately or in different combinations as a composite map (Figure 2).

Satellite imagery data is probably the most familiar example of raster data. This data can be complex and is pre-processed before it is able to be used on a computer GIS.

Scanned aerial photographs make a raster image of different tones on a computer screen. Here, each cell has a value according to its colour or tone.

Vector GIS

In a vector GIS, points, lines and areas are defined by x and y co-ordinates. A point may be defined by a pair of co-ordinates, e.g. 2,7 (x=2, y=7); a line is defined by a series of pairs. Areas have a series of pairs with the same start and end points (Figure 1). Information from a spreadsheet or database may be attached to any point, line or area.

Comparison of raster and vector GIS

Raster data is a regular grid of cells and the information about each cell is easy to manipulate on computer; but a large storage capacity is necessary if a detailed map is required. A single layer of 1024 by 1024 cells takes 1MB of storage space on computer.

Vector data is more complicated and time consuming to enter into the computer; but maps take up a much smaller amount of space. Maps may be made in great detail and with more accuracy.

Raster/vector conversion

Complex GIS can deal with data in both formats and transfer vector into raster (rasterisation) or raster into vector (vectorisation).

Getting maps into a GIS

Maps have to go through a digitising process in order to be stored in numerical form on computer. There are different methods, depending on whether the GIS accepts map data in raster or vector form.

Scanning

A scanner is a digitising device, rather like a photocopier, attached to a computer. When a copy of a map or photograph is fed into it, the image is saved on disk as a matrix of pixels producing a raster map.

Figure 1: Plotting data on a raster and vector maps.

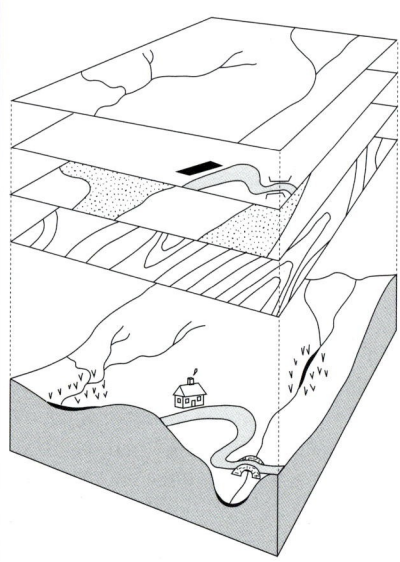

Figure 2: A map displayed as a series of overlays such as topography, roads or rivers. Source: Borough, 1987 by permission of Oxford University Press.

Digitising

This is the method for entering vector maps. A map is placed on a digitising tablet which is attached to the computer. Points, lines and areas on the map are outlined by hand with the cursor and saved on disk as a file of co-ordinates. Vector digitising may also be automated.

There are a number of different formats in which vector data may be saved, according to which GIS has been used for digitising.

Remote Sensing

Earth observation satellites have several scanners which sense energy reflected or emitted from the earth. Each scanner measures the energy for a given set of wavelengths and converts it into a digital signal which is transmitted to earth. These signals can be processed to produce a raster image. Up to three bands may be combined for images to show, for example, geology or land use. ■

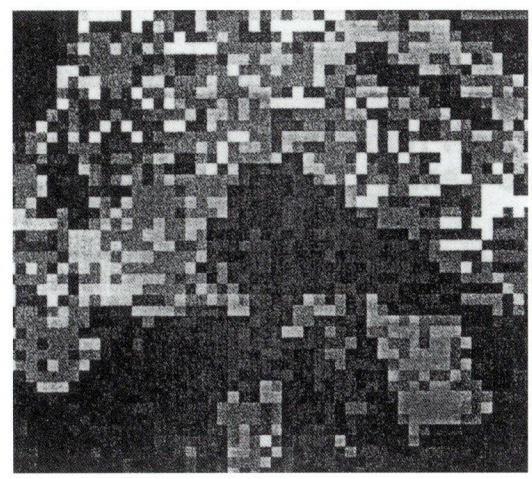

Figure 3: A map of land use produced by the Idrisi package.

References

Borough, P.A. (1987) *Principles of GIS for Land Resources Assessment.* Oxford: Oxford University Press.

Williams, A. (2000) 'Teaching and learning with geographical information systems', *Teaching Geography*, 25, 1, pp. [??].

> *Diana Freeman (The Advisory Unit: Computers in Education, Hatfield), David Green (University of Aberdeen) and David Hassell (BECTa) are members of the GIS section of the GA Information Technology Working Group.*

Low-cost GIS software

All websites should be prefixed with http://

AEGIS2 – PC-based software package for display, query and simple analysis of geographical data. Provided with sample digital maps of World (countries), Europe (regions) and UK (standard regions) as well as fieldwork examples. Can display point, line and area spatial data and attribute data in comma separated value format. Advisory Unit: Computers in Education, 126 Great North Road, Hatfield, Herts AL9 5JZ. Tel: 01707 266174; fax: 01707 273684; www.advisory-unit.org.uk

ArcView – The world's most popular desktop mapping and GIS software for *Windows 3.1, 95* and *NT, Apple Macintosh* and a range of other platforms. Provides a wide range of functions for data manipulation, management, query, analysis and display. May be extended with a number of additional, optional software modules. Comes supplied with sample data and tutorial programmes. Educational offers from Environmental Science Research Institute (UK), 23 Woodford Road, Watford, Hertfordshire WD1 1PB. Tel: 01923 210450; fax: 01923-210739; website: www.esriuk.com. Free ESRI software *ArcExplorer* (for *Windows '95* and *NT 4* only) is a pared-down version of ArcView which allows users to display and query a wide variety of standard data sources. It can also link to Internet map servers. *ArcView 1* is available for free (but stocks are limited) on compact disk, see website: www.esri.com/base/products/ArcExplorer/ArcExplorer.html

ATLAS Map Maker – a vector map and data display package that comes with outline maps of Europe and demographic statistical data. Import images in TIFF format and additional data from spreadsheets or databases. Contact: Adept Scientific, 6 Business Centre West, Avenue One, Letchworth, Herts SG6 2BR. Tel: 01462 480055.

Excel (version 7 onwards) – spreadsheet with mapping function. Allows production of choropleth maps from tabular data. Comes with a limited number of outline maps. Further maps can be imported in MapInfo format. Look on the Microsoft UK Education website for local dealers www.microsoft.com/uk/education/

Idrisi – Easy to use, yet competent software package for GIS, image processing and spatial statistics. Developed at the Graduate School of Clarke University specifically for educational purposes. Primarily designed for handling spatial data in grid (raster) format. A range of offers for educational institutions are available. Contact: The Idrisi Project, Clark Labs, Clark University, 950 Main Street, Worcester, MA 01610, USA Tel: 00 1 508 793 7526; fax: 00 1 508 793 8842; www.clarklabs.org/

MapInfo Professional – GIS and desk-top mapping software *for Windows 3.1, Windows '95* and *NT*. Capable of importing and exporting a wide range of digital map data formats and performing complex data manipulation, query and analysis operations. Educational licences, demo software and teaching packs are also available. Contact: MapInfo Corporation, Minton Place, Victoria Street, Windsor, Berkshire SL4 1EG. Tel: 01753 848200; e-mail: uk@mapinfo.com; www.mapinfo.com/software/index.html

Ordnance Survey – offers a wide range of digital map, aerial photograph and software products. Schools and colleges in local education authorities that have a Service Level Agreement with OS are able to obtain digital data via their authority. Further information can be found in Mapping Awareness. Contact: Ordnance Survey, Romsey Road, Southampton SO16 4GU. Tel: 023 8079 2906; www.ordsvy.gov.uk/home/index.html and look in the education section.

SCAMP – analysis and mapping package for the 1991 UK census. Provided with 17 categories of census data, census boundaries and base mapping. Census data can be displayed as choropleth maps and subjected to limited statistical analysis. Ordnance Survey Landline large scale digital map data may be imported and displayed as a backdrop to census data. Pebbleshore Ltd, Lewes Enterprise Centre,112 Malling Street, Lewes, Sussex BN7 2RJ. Tel: 01273 483890; fax: 01273 479645; www.pebbleshore.co.uk/

Source: Williams, 2000.

Where to find digitised maps

Vector and raster maps may be bought from commercial companies. These maps come in a variety of formats, and it is essential to check whether the GIS you want to use can accept the type of maps you need. Some GIS have an editor to draw maps to use within their own system.

Vector maps: the most common formats are Arc/Info (from Arc/Info GIS), DXF (from AutoCAD) or NTF (from Ordnance Survey). Local planning departments may distribute OS digitised maps to maintained schools under the Local Authority OS Service Level Agreement. The OS also has DXF and NTF maps for sample areas. Contact. Ordnance Survey Education Department, Romsey Road, Maybush, Southampton, SO9 4DH, for more details.

Raster maps: OS raster maps are available from MR-Data Graphics, Greenford House, 309 Ruislip Road, East Greenford, Middlesex, UB6 9BL.

Remotely-sensed images on disk for OS project maps and other areas are available from MJP Geopacks/Map Marketing, 92/104 Carnwath Road, London SW6 3HW. Tel: 0990 133168; e-mail: services@geopacks.com

Software and hardware

15 Visualisation software: a new aid to learning

The effects of flooding a valley can now be demonstrated on the computer screen. **David Holmes** *explains*

Developing ICT and geography

The last decade (1985-95) has seen an exponential increase in the numbers of computers both in school and at home. Coupled with this, there has been a huge expansion in software and learning aids applicable to geography. Teachers and students are feeling pressure to take advantage of the new technology. The problem lies with knowing where to start.

There is perhaps still uncertainty as how to maximise the integration of geography and ICT. Table 1 provides some examples. A photograph of a valley can be used to develop students' understanding of the effect of constructing a dam across a valley to create a reservoir, for example. This article describes how visualisation on a computer screen can be used as a further aid to learning about the impact of flooding on a valley.

Although there are benefits in using computers in geographical teaching, there is a danger that computers will become the focus of the lesson, rather than the geographical aim. Creating subject-based learning activities and experiences should be the focus of attention in any ICT situation. There is a natural tendency to concentrate on a computer and to become immersed in the intricacies of software rather than considering the broader aims of the activity. Developers are now accepting that avoidance of such a situation is problematic. An active learning technique focuses on the development of (students') preconceived ideas, bolstering them with experiential themes. This approach differs from many conventional packages, where the software presents the ordinary view of a topic. The traditional approach starts from the position of an expert (or program) rather than building up from where the learners begin (Riley *et al.*, 1990).

It is the active or open-learning strategy that appears most suitable. IT in geography seems most successful when used to supplement learning materials and not always as the focal point for learning. However, these new technology developments are exciting and should form a stimulus to encourage increased student participation and in turn generate wider considerations. A technique of marrying ICT and geography has been successfully developed for fieldwork teaching at Preston Montford, one of the Field Studies Council's residential centres. This article is based around the framework of a teaching day which incorporates ICT into the learning activity.

Carding Mill Valley or Ashes Hollow: The case for flooding

New geography syllabuses are increasingly asking students to consider conflicts over resources at various scales. The revised Order requires that students 'consider the issues which arise from people's interactions with their environments'. Students should be made aware of concepts such as landscape assessment, stewardship and resource conservation. Carding Mill Valley and Ashes Hollow in south Shropshire provide good examples for a local scale

Geographical aims	Traditional method	Incorporation of ICT
Student enquiry to develop geographical skills. To deepen understanding of environmental and spatial relationships.	Collection of primary and secondary data. Undertake a broad enquiry approach to a topic. People-environment relationships and analysing changes over time including location decisions, e.g. using photographs.	Data logging, spreadsheets, new graphing techniques. Ability to handle large volumes of data. Relationships become real and affordable through new techniques, e.g. *Vistapro*.

Table 1: **Examples of the incorporation of ICT into geography.**

When faced with large areas, land managers generally find it difficult to assess the quality of a site. The word 'quality' implies that a value judgement is being made by a person or by a group of people, and hence the criteria for assessing conservation value cannot be considered as completely scientific. In order to assist you in making a valid judgement of a site, before and following reservoir development, you may find it useful to consider the following factors:

	Before	After
Size		
Diversity		
Naturalness		
Rarity		
Typicalness		
Fragility		
Recorded History		
Position in an ecological unit		
Potential value		
Intrinsic appeal		

You must devise your own method of scoring each consideration. *There are no right or wrong answers*. However, you can use your judgement as evidence of degradation or enhancement of the site as the result of reservoir development.

Table 2: **Assessment of conservation value: Recording sheet.**

route to enquiry. The scheme of the day is presented through a general aim: **To investigate the conflicts of interest that arise from managing an upland area as a water resource.** *Since the activity is hypothetical in its design, it is transferable between various situations and geographical regions.*

Students are briefed about the need to increase water supplies in the south Shropshire region. They are presented with statistics relating to average daily water consumption per person in the UK and asked to consider ways in which Severn Trent (the water company responsible for supply in the region) can increase the supply of water in the area. It is then suggested to them that the most suitable method of meeting future water demands will be to construct a reservoir in the south Shropshire Hills. Students are advised that Severn Trent have examined a number of possible sites and conclude that either Carding Mill Valley or Ashes Hollow will present the best opportunity for the development of an impoundment.

This method of leading students through a series of pre-determined decisions has proved to be a successful route by which to present the introduction. This session is followed by a visit to the sites where students are required to evaluate suitability for impoundment.

Fieldwork at each proposed site is focused around a number of objectives: deciding whether the water quality meets the standards required by the relevant water company; ensuring that there is the necessary discharge to fill a dam; and evaluating the environmental impact of such a development on the valley. The first two aims are relatively easy to assess. Water quality is determined through biological testing (kick-sampling of macro-invertebrates) and by simple chemical tests (NO_3^-, NH_4 and pH) using test strips or indicator pens. Approximate discharge is measured by calculating flow-rate and channel cross-sectional area.

The environmental impacts of a dam are harder to appraise. One method is to use Ratcliffe's (1977) criteria and to consider site characteristics including size, diversity, naturalness, position in an ecological unit, etc., applied to the site before and after impoundment. However, students must be briefed about the complexities of such a methodology and allowed to make their own (subjective) decisions surrounding impact. To aid the students in their assessment, a simple table is used (Table 2). This information is supplemented by field sketches and photographs.

Following the site visit, students are organised into appropriate role-play groups. Examples include entrepreneurs (future developers including

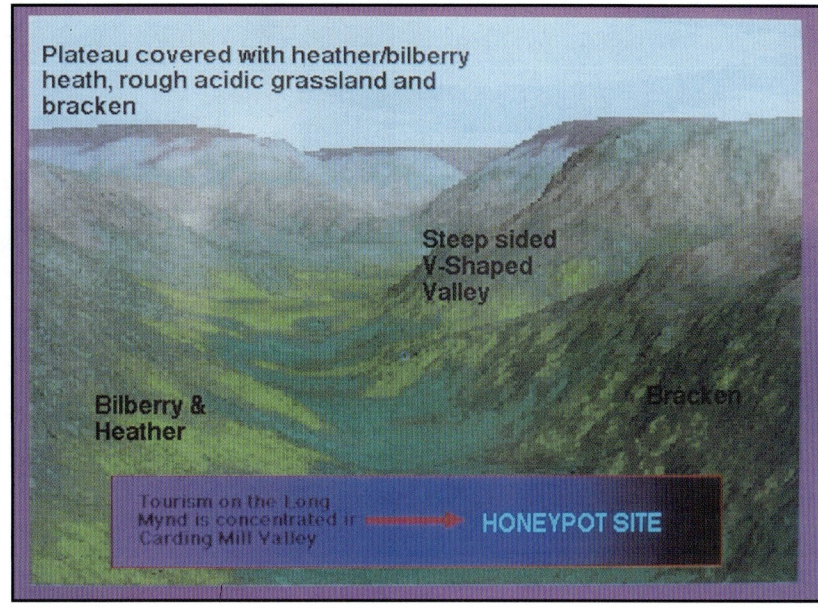

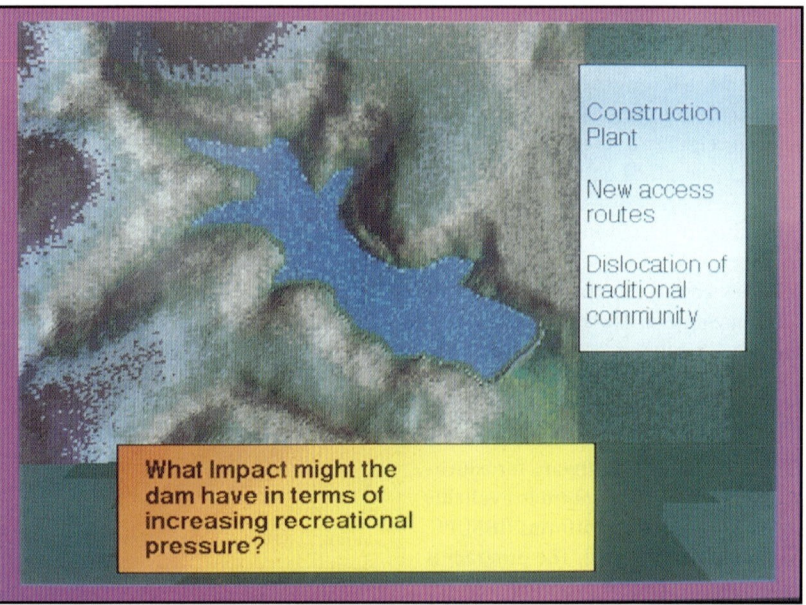

Figure 3: The rendered images of Carding Mill Valley.

financiers), water officers, recreation officers, conservationists, local residents and farmers. Ideally there are equal numbers of groups for and against the development. The students are then instructed to use all the available resources (both primary and secondary data) to formulate an argument for their working party. The results are best presented through an organised debate, in which students decide the best location and the optimum dam size.

Integration of computer visualisation

The revised Order makes reference to geographical skills, including fieldwork and the use of ICT. Computer visualisation can be used to experience 'alternative images of place and environment' and to 'deepen students' understanding of environmental and spatial relationships' (GA/NCET, 1994).

A landscape generator program, *Vistapro*, is used to make pictures of real landscapes from *Digital Elevation Model* (DEM) data. DEM files contain three-dimensional elevation data that Vistapro uses to render, or draw, landscapes. The pictures are simulated landscapes 'in their natural state' and can be viewed from a practically infinite combination of heights, angles and distances. The DEM files are easily loaded and a simple, rendered image is produced within a number of minutes. However, large images (in terms of pixel numbers) with high levels of detail require a longer rendering time. The rendered image can also be customised; in the case of Carding Mill Valley (for which data has been obtained), an artificial bund has been added to one end of the valley and subsequently flooded to a predetermined depth. Preparation time for this particular simulation was about half a day.

Another program (included on the *Vistapro* CD-ROM), *Flight-path*, can be used in conjunction with *Vistapro* to create a fly-through animation of the simulated landscape. This type of simulation requires a relatively fast computer (a 486 PC or equivalent) and the task is very processor-intensive as each individual rendered image is 'stitched' together. A 30-second animation requires about 250 frames to achieve fluid movement. The results, however, are worthwhile as a simulated flight through a virtual landscape is both astonishing and dramatic.

Some of the larger retailers offer discounts on their software for educational customers; *Vistapro* is available for the three main platforms (IBM/PC, Macintosh and Acorn). The program is also easy to operate with 'pull-down'-style menus and a comprehensive user manual. DEMs of the UK for use with

Photo: Richard Greenhill.

Vistapro are currently available for a number of regions, including the Lake District, North Wales and parts of the Scottish Highlands.

Vistapro has proved to be an effective and reasonably priced visualisation tool. The software is used in the classroom environment as a computer screen 'slide show'. The 'slide-show' utility, available in a number of software packages, allows the rendered landscapes (saved as separate picture files) to be viewed as a series of images which are then annotated with relevant information (Figure 1). Animated sequences can also be incorporated into the series of slides. Students respond enthusiastically to rendered landscape images, which have promoted discussion about all aspects of impoundment, including loss of the upland wildscape and creation of new wetland ecosystems. Fly-through or animated images are most popular with students, allowing them to feel that they are really experiencing the scenery.

Initial assessment of the technique provides promising results. Students have provided mainly positive comments about the new technology, although some have suggested that it should be made more interactive. Rendered images following impoundment tend to make the valley appear more attractive, giving advantage to those groups arguing for the valley's development. Further consideration of these points is required.

Conclusion

The use of visualisation software in teaching is still in its infancy. However, with such positive reactions to the simulations so far, there seems to be little doubt that it can be further developed and enhanced for wider applications. The technique is not restricted to geographers and environmental scientists: there are many other potential uses for this visualisation software, including biology and geology. Planners working with local authorities may find visualisation can be used as an analytical tool within the framework of Environmental Impact Assessment. ■

Acknowledgement
The author wishes to thank the National Trust for information on Carding Mill Valley, which the Trust owns and manages.

Further information
Educational group visits to Carding Mill Valley must be pre-booked through the Education Officer, Chris Stratten, Tel: 01694 72463.

A teachers' resource pack *The Long Mynd* (1999) which contains useful information for key stage 4 and 16+ students is now available. The pack costs £9.95 (inc VAT, plus £1.20 p+p) from The Education Officer, The National Trust, Chalet Pavilion, Carding Mill Valley, Church Stretton, Shropshire SY6 6JG.

References
GA/NCET (1994) *Geography – A Student's Entitlement for IT*. Sheffield/Coventry: GA/NCET.
Ratcliffe, D.A. (ed) (1977) *A Nature Conservation Review. Vols 1 and 2*. Cambridge: Cambridge University Press.
Riley et al. (1990) *Design for Active Learning with Hypercard*. London: Kings College, University of London.
Smith, D. (1995) 'Shaping our future', *Macformat*, 20 January, p. 51.

David Holmes is Assistant Warden at Preston Montford Field Centre, Shropshire, Tel: 01743 850380; e-mail: dave.holmes@telinco-co.uk.

ICT training

16 Developing novice teacher ICT competence

Liz Newcombe describes her research into using geographical information systems in a PGCE geography course (1999)

The current competency in Information and Communications Technology (ICT) expected of newly qualified teachers is to:

'xii. have a working knowledge of information technology (IT) to a standard equivalent to Level 8 in the National Curriculum for pupils, and understand the contribution that IT makes to their specialist subject[s]'
(DfEE, 1997, p. 8)

This new requirement presents a challenge to initial teacher education given that novice teachers spend 24 out of 36 weeks in schools, where it is recognised that good ICT practice is not the norm (DES, 1988, 1992). This article explores one strategy utilised in the Postgraduate Certificate in Education (PGCE) course at the University of Birmingham. This course initially focuses on one application, geographical information systems (GIS), utilising strategies to develop professional as well as personal competence.

The new requirements

Novice teachers must satisfy level 8 of the National Curriculum for Information Technology:

'Pupils select the appropriate IT facilities for specific tasks, taking into account ease of use and suitability for purpose. They design and implement systems for others to use. They design successful means of capturing and, if necessary, preparing information for computer processing. When assembling devices that respond to data from sensors, they describe how feedback might improve the performance of the system. They discuss in an informed way, the social, economic, ethical and moral issues raised by IT' (DfE, 1995, p. 7).

However, the control element of this level description need not be explored with novice teachers if it does not have direct relevance to their subject specialism(s) as is the case with geography.

The ICT requirements for newly qualified teachers (DfEE, 1997) place the following demands on novice teachers to:

- use a range of generic software demonstrating key functions (e.g. sorting, searching, graphical output, modelling)
- use and evaluate electronic sources
- combine text/images to prepare material for student use
- copy and paste within and between applications
- select software appropriate to task and be aware of subject specific software
- have familiarity in file management
- collect/structure data for later retrieval
- have an understanding of data validity
- design student lessons with associated documentation.

Why focus on GIS?
GIS is:

'... a powerful set of tools for collecting, storing, retrieving at will, transforming, and displaying spatial data from the real world for a particular set of purposes'
(Burrough, 1986, p. 6).

This software is at the very heart of geography. Given that the focus of GIS is spatial analysis and mapping its relevance and value is clear. Linking data to maps, interrogating the data, determining appropriate methods of display and most importantly analysing this spatial output has the potential to transform the teaching and learning of geography at all levels.

Focusing on one application of direct relevance to the subject does appear to run counter to the view that novice teachers need to gain familiarity with a range of generic and subject specific software. In selecting software for novice teachers to use it is critical that they have the opportunity to develop higher order competencies in two areas. These are working across applications and devising systems for student to use. It may be more appropriate initially to use an in-depth study of one application to explore the plethora of skills

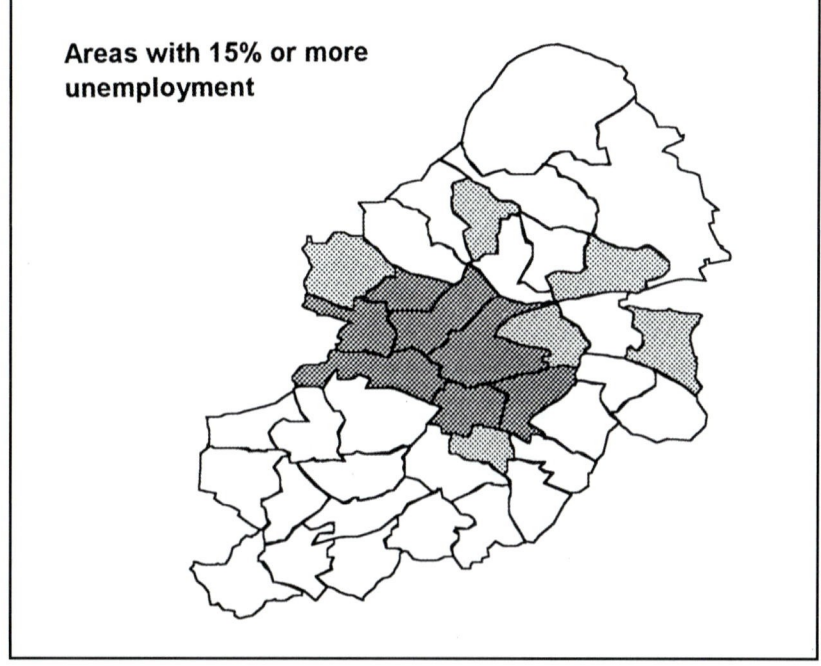

Figure 1: The mapped result of using AEGIS2 to perform a simple search for areas of high unemployment in Birmingham.

Week no.	Focus of session
2	Two introductory sessions ■ familiarity with functions ■ classroom examples ■ setting up a simple GIS
5	Classroom observation ■ small group focus ■ teaching and learning
3-10	Optional sessions ■ exploration at own pace ■ support in development
7-11	Practical assignment ■ design, plan and evaluate a GIS ■ classroom activity

Figure 2: Timescale of GIS experiences.

Figure 3: A novice teacher pair plan their practical assignment. *Photo:* Liz Newcombe.

concomitant with successful implementation of ICT in the classroom. As one mentor teacher commented:

'I think clearly [the novice teachers] were better this year because they'd had IT sessions with a focus at the university and that made a difference ... I think even through one package you'll be enskilling them to use so many other packages'.

This view is also supported by Diana Freeman, a GIS expert[1]:

'An in-depth study, concentrating on one flexible program such as AEGIS, is the only way to successfully put across these points. It is only when students are actively engaged in a long task that they achieve a higher level of understanding of the opportunities afforded by open-ended software. The learning curve is a steep one, but once the critical stage has been reached, the students are able to take charge of the learning process and apply it with confidence' (Freeman, personal communication).

What is AEGIS?

AEGIS is a simple geographical system, in which:

■ maps are linked with data from spreadsheets or databases,

■ maps can be created in the editor,

■ Ordnance Survey digital tiles and scanned images can be imported,

■ data is linked to points, lines or areas on the map,

■ the user can generate bar or line graphs, flow-lines, pie charts or choropleth maps,

■ questions can be used to select data (see, for example, Figure 1), and

■ distances and areas can be measured.

The 'building blocks' for professional development

Historically, evaluation of the success of ICT in initial teacher education has often been in terms of novice teachers' perceived improvement in confidence and competence to use ICT personally. However, it is erroneous to equate personal competence with professional competence in the classroom. A pilot study of PGCE geography novice teachers at the University of Birmingham in 1994-95 demonstrated that whilst most novices registered an improvement in personal competence, the vast majority made little use of ICT in their teaching and many felt insecure about its classroom use.

By narrowing the initial focus of ICT provision to one application, this provided the opportunity to explore a progression of activities designed to move novice teachers from personal users in the application to professional competence in the planning, delivery and evaluation of classroom practice.

Many studies highlight that positive classroom experiences promote subsequent ICT use by novice teachers. Davis (1992), for instance, considers that novices working with children in the training institutions and novices observing teachers working with children in schools are two key factors. Some researchers place value on these classroom experiences occurring early on in the course (Dunn and Ridgway, 1991; Monaghan, 1993).

Introducing an element of compulsion in the use of ICT through a practical assignment is another avenue that has been explored. Whiteman (1992) argues that some novice teachers need 'extrinsic motivation' to start using ICT but develop their 'intrinsic motivation' once they have overcome fears. Whilst some researchers report

Developing a GIS

■ topic identification with mentor

■ drawing base map or utilising existing one

■ entering data into spreadsheet

■ linking map to data

Designing a classroom activity

■ structuring/sequencing geographical learning

■ developing associated support materials

Delivering GIS activity

■ classroom use with small group of students in first few weeks of teaching

■ reflection and evaluation

Outcomes

■ early success stimulates further ICT classroom use

Figure 4: Stages in the assignment.

Table 1: Awareness/use of GIS.

Awareness level	Year group 1995-96 (%)	1996-97 (%)
No awareness	30.0	26.4
Basic awareness	30.0	58.8
Theoretical awareness	35.0	38.3
Practical experience	15.0	11.8

Table 2: Attitudinal responses to GIS.

	Year group 1995-96 (%)	1996-97 (%)
I am pleased to have undertaken some GIS		
Agree/strongly agree	85.0	100.0
Tend to agree	10.0	0.0
Using GIS can stimulate pupil interest in a topic		
Agree/strongly agree	90.0	91.2
Tend to agree	10.0	8.8
Using GISs enables students to perform tasks not otherwise possible		
Agree/strongly agree	65.0	61.8
Tend to agree	25.0	29.4
GIS has no relevance to the secondary school classroom		
Disagree/strongly disagree	95.0	100.0
Tend to disagree	5.0	0.0
I would like to see GIS abandoned from the PGCE course		
Disagree/strongly disagree	95.0	100.0
Tend to disagree	5.0	0.0
GIS are too difficult for teachers and children to understand		
Disagree/strongly disagree	75.0	73.5
Tend to disagree	25.0	26.5

some anxiety in novices, the overwhelming evidence is that novice teachers persevere more with an assignment focus (Simmons and Wild, 1992), and develop a more positive attitude to ICT and a greater willingness to use ICT in their teaching.

A programme of work was devised (Figure 2) which was informed by this earlier research. An introduction was provided in two 90 minute sessions. In the first of these novice teachers gained familiarity in using GIS, experiencing concrete classroom activities and utilising a variety of scales and different types of display (e.g. choropleth maps, pie and bar charts, flow lines). The second session explored the 'mechanics' of the package such as setting up a simple GIS and developing macros (a series of instructions which can be executed in a single action). This introduction was followed by classroom observation of ICT with small groups. The nature of teaching and learning was the observation focus. Finally, novice teachers undertook a practical assignment in pairs, devising a classroom activity with comprehensive documentation which was then introduced to a small group of students (Figure 3).

A half-day in-service training was provided in advance for mentor teachers. The purpose of the in-service training was to gain familiarity with AEGIS, discuss reasons for course changes and develop strategies to support novices in undertaking the assignment. An emphasis was placed on support of a more general nature rather than in ICT *per se*, for example:

- help in identifying a suitable topic;
- the structuring and sequencing of learning (see Figure 4);
- readability levels of associated documentation; and
- classroom management issues.

This strategy was designed to raise mentor teachers' confidence as they do not necessarily identify ICT as a particular strength.

Main findings

Novice teacher background in GIS

While much literature purports GIS value for enhancing spatial analysis, it appears from this study that GIS have not yet impacted to any significant degree on undergraduate study. Table 1 indicates that in both year groups of the main study, less than 20 per cent agreed or strongly agreed that they had any practical experience, although roughly one-third had a theoretical awareness (35 per cent in 1995-96, 38.3 per cent in 1996-97). Basic awareness was substantially increased in the second year group (58.8 per cent compared with 30 per cent). It was somewhat surprising to discover that a significant proportion of each year group (30 per cent in 1995-96, 26.4 per cent in 1996-97), had no experience of GIS at all, even to the extent of ever having heard of their existence.

In many respects, having had some awareness of GIS applicability without the opportunity to personally experience its use, might be more of a stimulus for interest at PGCE level than having utilised advanced packages beforehand. The reactions of the two groups suggest that it was perceived as a new and exciting medium.

Novice teacher attitudes to GIS

While those committed to GIS in secondary education may expound the applicability and value of their use, it is only if the classroom teacher can see their potential value and appropriateness that they will become more universally used. All novices reject the view that GIS have no relevance to the secondary classroom with a majority in each year (1995-96, 1996-97) at the strongest level of disagreement (see Table 2). All novices disagreed that GIS are too difficult for teachers and children to understand. However, only one-fifth in each year disagreed at the strongest level which suggests that there is not full conviction. Given that AEGIS2 must be regarded as a simplistic GIS, this result perhaps calls into question the likely receptivity towards more complex commercial packages.

Following their course experiences, novice teachers perceived the main strengths of AEGIS2 to be:

- the motivational impact which prompts students to become more engaged in their work;
- the ability to present data graphically, experiment with alternative methods of graphical display and generate graphics far more quickly to thereby concentrate on analysis;

Table 3: Evaluation of some ICT course components.

	Year group 1995-96 (%)	1996-97 (%)
Introduction to GIS		
Useful/very useful	50.0	94.2
Tending to be useful	45.0	5.9
Classroom observation		
Useful/very useful	68.4	73.5
Tending to be useful	26.3	17.6
Practical assignment		
Useful/very useful	80.0	91.2
Tending to be useful	10.0	8.8
Spreadsheets		
Useful/very useful	30.0	73.5
Tending to be useful	15.0	14.7

Table 4: Outcomes identified by trainees.

	Year group 1995-96 (%)	1996-97 (%)
Positive outcomes		
Greater awareness of GIS	20.4	18.4
Practical use of GIS	19.4	19.6
Greater confidence in using ICT	16.1	17.2
Designing support materials	16.1	16.6
Positive ICT class experience	15.1	18.4
More familiarity with *Windows*	9.7	8.0
Other	3.2	1.8
Negative outcomes		
Frustrated by the software	51.4	31.8
Time consuming to develop	25.7	61.4
Less confident in using ICT	2.9	0.0
Limited value for teaching and learning	2.9	2.3
Other	14.3	4.5

- the visualisation of data in its spatial setting which aids understanding;

- the access to a wealth of data enhancing students' powers of analysis which proves difficult, if not impossible, without this medium;

- the ability of the GIS to enable students to become autonomous and creative in their own learning.

The impact of course change

The vast majority of novice teachers valued the classroom observation of a teacher using GIS. It provided some reassurance that GIS could work in the classroom and could interest and motivate students. But more importantly, the small group focus appeared to provide a 'safe environment' in which novice teachers could comfortably explore, and gain insights into the role of the teacher in this context to inform their future practice.

However, not all classroom observation was viewed positively. This was the case in 1995-96 when one group carried out the session much later in the autumn term (Table 3). This appears to support other research findings (Dunn and Ridgway, 1991; Monaghan, 1993) which emphasise the importance of this experience occurring early on in the course.

The practical assignment was identified by novice teachers as the most valuable ICT input in each year with an extremely strong level of support although apprehension did surface in the early stages of the project. Later the success emanating from the work in the classroom took on more significance, particularly with novices who had registered greatest limitations in their own abilities. An element of compulsion had been critical in getting many involved in using ICT. Working in a pair appeared to be a supportive strategy and operating with small groups rather than, necessarily, whole classes had also been important.

The positive outcomes of the assignment far outweighed negative feedback by both mentor teachers and novices (Table 4). Positive outcomes identified were varied in both years, suggesting that it was not just the GIS experience but a range of professional skills relating to ICT which were developing. In 1995-96, the over-riding negative outcome for novices had been a 'dissatisfaction in the software' (Table 4). This was superseded in 1996-97 by 'time for development' which supported the researcher's view that AEGIS2 was far more user-friendly for novices than the original version.

In the second year of the main study, the results had been even more conclusive in relation to the assignment with 61.8 per cent viewing it as 'very useful' compared with 35 per cent in the previous year. The nature of the software had improved which may have contributed to this. It is also suggested that more active involvement of mentor teachers in supporting novices in the planning played a part (1995-96 50 per cent involved compared with 70.6 per cent in 1996-97), with those still reluctant to be involved often new to the partnership.

At a basic level, these early experiences ensured a minimum entitlement for all novice teachers in observing, planning and delivering the use of ICT in geography. The element of compulsion, by their own admission, was critical in getting many involved in using ICT. Additionally, novices gained ICT experience irrespective of school placement or mentor teacher expertise. However, for many novices, these early experiences were a 'kick start' for further development. Personal satisfaction and 'early success' stimulated many to do further work in the classroom.

Effecting change – towards a symbiosis?

Many researchers have argued the importance of closer collaboration between initial teacher education institutions and partnership schools in ICT provision (Monaghan, 1993; NCET, 1993) given limitations in practice in many partnership schools. Is there evidence within this research that a collaborative approach has effected change in novice teacher experience, mentor teacher competency and response to ICT, and departmental practice?

Novice teacher experience has improved significantly over the three-year period in terms of their frequency of classroom use of ICT. Their feedback on the value of the placement school in supporting their professional development in ICT has shown a marked improvement from the first to the second year of the main study. However, it would be erroneous to lay full credit for this at the door of changes made since some schools are clearly moving on independently. The researcher's observations in the schools visited are that, in the majority of this sample, ICT is now clearly on the agenda for professional development. This is noticeable even in schools where this would not have been the case previously. ICT has moved from being an 'option' which could be explored to one which needs to be undertaken. It is only fair to comment that this sample does not include any schools new to the partnership.

Mentor teachers' perceived competence to support novice teachers in planning/delivering the use of ICT also indicates improvement from the first to the second year of the main study. Over three-quarters of the teachers now feel positively towards this role. Some of the less confident mentor teachers have developed more positive self-perceptions. These mentors are clearly, from the researcher's observations, offering more practical support. Providing a focus, continuing emphasis on the non-ICT elements of support and 'the second time around' may have contributed to this. However, again, other factors may well have impacted. While the overall positive response from mentor teachers to the GIS assignment was slightly lower than the previous year, this does appear to reflect a less positive response from new partnership schools. The vast majority of schools who have participated over the two years (81.8 per cent) now rate it as 'very useful'. This does suggest a 'lead in' time before the impact of change is appreciated.

In some schools, there was a clear drive from the start to 'embed' the novice teachers' GIS work into the curriculum so that it would benefit whole year groups and subsequent years. Inevitably, this has tended to happen in schools where the mentor teacher is a 'technological enthusiast' and where ICT is already making a valuable contribution to the geography department. However, this is not exclusively the case. In one school, for instance, the department now has four or five GIS activities, none of which were directly developed by the department. The mentor teacher would describe herself as an ICT novice and the department, while well resourced, does not otherwise utilise ICT to any great extent. This scale of development would not typify the partnership schools where ICT does not already have a high profile. However, it is significant that a number of schools are utilising work from previous years and commenting in evaluation on the value of the work produced by novice teachers for the department. The work has had least impact in schools which are new to the partnership, where computers are too limited to use AEGIS2, and/or where the mentor teacher is a 'technological antagonist'.

A key element for the success of this partnership appears to be in persuading mentor teachers that the benefit of this work is two-fold. Firstly, it enhances the professional development of novice teachers; and secondly, it contributes to ICT curriculum innovation in departments. In those departments where the latter has been recognised, it has greater impact for novice teachers who have been encouraged by increased departmental use. Clearly, those mentor teachers with greater ICT competence themselves have realised these benefits quickly but it is clear that a widening group of schools is moving in this direction.

Conclusion

This research suggests that other geography educators within initial teacher education would be well advised to consider the place of GIS within their programmes. More importantly, it confirms other research which places importance on an element of compulsion within provision and of the need for this to be developed early on in the course for maximum impact. Rather than a programme preoccupied with a breadth of ICT experience, research needs to focus on the necessary 'building blocks' to move novice teachers from personal users in any application to competent classroom practitioners. Historically, there has been an underevaluation of the importance of an induction in ICT in the formative pre-service training of teachers. If this is not redressed, ICT in geography will continue to be seen as 'for the occasional enrichment' (Burkhill, 1996, p. 221) rather than as an enabler for advanced learning opportunities. ∎

Note

1. Diana Freeman is Director of AU Enterprises Ltd – the producers of AEGIS2, the particular GIS used with novice teachers. AEGIS2 software is available from AU Enterprises Ltd, 126 Great North Road, Hatfield, Hertfordshire AL9 5JZ. Tel: 01707 266714.

Acknowledgement

The author would like to thank the staff and students at Swanshurst School, Birmingham for their continuing co-operation with this project.

References

Burrough, P.A. (1986) *Principles of Geographical Information Systems for Land Resources Assessment*. Oxford: Clarendon Press.

Burkhill, S. (1996) 'Trends in school geography and information technology' in Rawling, E.M. and Daugherty, R.A. (eds) *Geography into the Twenty-first Century*. Chichester: Wiley.

Davis, N. (1992) 'Information Technology in United Kingdom Initial Teacher Education', *Journal of Information Technology for Teacher Education*, 1, pp. 7-21.

DES (1988) *A Survey of Information Technology within Initial Teacher Training in the Public Sector. A report by HMI*. London: HMSO.

DES (1992) *Information Technology in Initial Teacher Education Two Years after the Trotter Report. A report by HMI*. London: HMSO.

Department for Education (1995) *Information Technology in the National Curriculum*. London: HMSO.

Department for Education and Employment (DfEE) (1997) *Requirements for courses of Initial Teacher Training. Annex B: Initial Teacher Training Curriculum for the use of Information and Communications Technology in subject teaching* (Circular no. 4/97). London: HMSO.

Dunn, S. and Ridgway, J. (1991) 'Naked into the world: IT experiences on a final primary school teaching practice – a second survey', *Journal of Computer Assisted Learning*, 7, pp. 229-40.

Monaghan, J. (1993) 'IT in mathematics initial teacher training – factors influencing school experience', *Journal of Computer Assisted Learning*, 9, pp. 149-60.

NCET (1993) *Initial Teacher Education and New Technology: Project INTENT final report*. Coventry: NCET.

Simmons, C. and Wild, P. (1992) 'New forms of student teacher learning', *Educational Review*, 44, 1, pp. 31-40.

Whiteman, S. (1992) *IT Works For Us: Raising the quality of student teachers' school-based and school-focused IT experience*. Coventry: NCET.

Dr Liz Newcombe was formerly Lecturer in Geography Education in the School of Education at the University of Birmingham.

ICT training

17 Will you get some training?

David Hassell looks at the £230 million scheme for training teachers in the use of information and communications technology (1999)

Introduction

In November 1998, the Prime Minister, Tony Blair, and the Secretary of State for Education, David Blunkett, announced further details of the Government's strategy for developing the National Grid for Learning (NGfL). Their announcement provided an overview of the initiatives in information and communications technology (ICT) between 1998 and the year 2002. The initiatives involve an investment of more than £1 billion and are designed to meet the Government's targets in ICT. The Government expects that by 2002:

- serving teachers should generally feel confident, and be competent to teach, using ICT within the curriculum;
- all schools, colleges, universities and libraries and as many community centres as possible should be connected to the NGfL;
- most school leavers should have a good understanding of ICT;
- the UK should be a centre for excellence in the development of networks;
- general administrative communications to schools should be electronic, not paper-based.

Many people think the NGfL is the website of the same name. The title, however, refers to the development of the infrastructure, skills and materials which will underpin a renewed learning society. The initiative intends to provide lifelong opportunities with a range of elements which address further, higher and adult learning (NGfL, 1997, 1998a). However, the most funding is going to the compulsory education sector (schools) where there are primarily five elements to the NGfL:

1. Standards Fund grants (over £700 million between 1998 and 2002) to be spent on connecting and upgrading school ICT equipment.
2. The managed services initiative which will support cost-effective purchasing of certified, appropriate equipment and services.
3. The development of a NGfL website along with Virtual Teacher Centres for England, Scotland, Wales and Northern Ireland.
4. Funding for librarian training and digitisation of content.
5. New Opportunities Fund (NOF) training for teachers.

The last item in this list and the opportunities it offers are the focus of the remainder of this article.

The scheme

The New Opportunities Fund supports teacher training in the use of ICT to enhance subject teaching and learning. The initiative has £230 million of investment in this sector over the next three years. The high profile launch of the training initiative, which is co-ordinated and managed by the Teacher Training Agency (TTA), included a statement to the effect that *all* teachers would be trained. However, the approach currently being used is based on a deficit model so, although there is the appearance of *opportunity* for training for all teachers, in reality those teachers who already meet the ICT expectations may not need any training.

Background

In 1998, the TTA developed the *National Curriculum for ICT* in initial teacher education (ITE) which is being introduced in teacher training institutions during the 1998-99 academic year. This is the first plank in the training plan and is intended to ensure that newly-qualified teachers enter schools with the necessary ICT skills. Using the ITE curriculum as a basis, the New Opportunities Fund supports ICT training to serving teachers. These are detailed in a booklet from the TTA, entitled *The Use of ICT in Subject Teaching* (TTA, 1999). The principle aim of the ICT training is to equip teachers with the necessary knowledge, skills and understanding to make sound decisions about when and when not to use ICT, as well as how to use ICT effectively in teaching any subject. The expected outcomes are described in two sections:

- A Effective teaching and assessment methods.
- B Teachers' knowledge and understanding of, and competence with, ICT.

Discussion with heads and teachers indicates that many models of implementation are being developed. As the training scheme is not compulsory some educators may feel that they are happy to let this initiative pass them by. However, a clear message on the importance of all teachers receiving the necessary training can be found in the Green Paper *Teachers Meeting the Challenge of Change*:

> 'the need to emphasise the need for teachers to be equipped with good ICT skills, and introduce a contractual duty for teachers to keep their skills up-to-date' (DfEE, 1998b).

The New Opportunities Fund scheme allows teachers and schools to identify individual ICT training needs and then plan its provision.

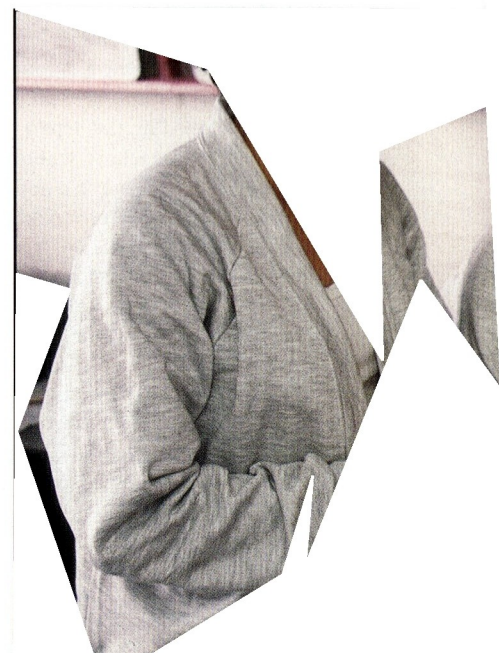

The structure of the scheme

The scheme will run over three financial years – with schools being the locus of planning for teachers. The first two elements of the scheme are now in place. They are:

- a process to accredit training providers, and
- the development of needs identification materials for teachers.

A wide range of organisations have applied to be accredited – either individually or in groups (over 30 were successful in the role of training English teachers). The TTA has developed two sets of needs identification materials designed to enable individual teachers and schools to identify their training needs and plan a training programme. The first paper-based materials will be in schools during April 1999, with multimedia materials available in the summer term. Using these and a formula for funding teachers and schools can plan their needs and apply to a local administrator to start training. Schools will not receive direct funding, instead they will receive the training which will be paid for from the New Opportunities Fund. When the training is complete, and the teachers and administrator are satisfied with the provision, the training is approved and the provider is paid from a central source. More details on the roles of the different groups are provided below.

TTA role

The TTA have developed and will retain oversight of the whole scheme. The Agency is also responsible for its effective operation. In this context, the main role for the TTA is monitoring existing providers and accrediting new ones (future opportunities for further providers to become accredited are planned), developing its expected outcomes needs identification and exemplification materials.

The training provider

Those training providers which have already been accredited are developing their courses and the associated materials. It is important to realise that the training will not take place as 'days out of school'. Instead it will comprise a range of components that will normally take place over a period of time mainly in school. Existing providers have stated which parts of the country and subjects they will cover and the training approach they intend to use. Some are heavily based on distance learning, others have local support and personal contact, and all use ICT for communications between the trainer and teacher. As soon as the detailed lists of providers and courses are prepared they will be distributed to all schools.

The school

The school will receive the needs identification materials and will be expected to ensure that all teachers (and school librarians) use them to identify their training needs. Schools intending to apply for training must have sufficient ICT equipment to enable teachers to follow the course, communicate with course providers and develop their skills. Poorly equipped schools will need to wait until they have obtained NGfL Standards Fund equipment (Ask your LEA NGfL co-ordinator/ICT adviser/inspector about how the Standard's Fund is organised in your authority). Schools with ICT provision will need to illustrate that they have an effective ICT development plan to support their training plan. This might be spread across the three coming financial years.

A key element of implementing the plan will be to identify training providers and appropriate training for each teacher. **The choice is down to the school**, but it must consider both the quality of the subject expertise and the training methodology. The next stage will be to apply to a local administrator (see below) to start training. Once training has commenced the school should monitor what individual teachers are receiving and what is expected. On completion, the school should reach agreement with the provider that the training has been completed satisfactorily. The school should also ensure that all its teachers will meet the expected outcomes by 2002.

The local administrator

A local administrator, probably the LEA, in each area will act as an **independent** agent of the TTA to manage the process of ICT training. Schools prepare their plans and apply to a nominated contact in the LEA. This contact checks against TTA criteria whether the school is ready to start training and act as a link in the administration process. Once training is complete the administrator and school must agree that it has been done satisfactorily, so the administrator can release payment to the provider.

Your role

The main issue for you as a geography teacher is to ensure that you can obtain the necessary training with the most appropriate trainer. The 31 existing training providers may propose to train in particular geographical areas and/or in specific subjects, this will limit you and your school's choice of provider. Furthermore, because geography can use ICT in a variety of ways it is unlikely that providers will cover everything – such an approach would considerably dilute the training offered. To match your requirements as closely as possible, you and your school are advised to look carefully at the subject expertise and the type of geography courses offered, along with the method of delivery.

The role of the GA

As evidence of the range of geography training builds up, the Geographical Association plans to report on geography providers in future issues of *Teaching Geography*. To do this, it is vital that we receive feedback from you on your training experiences. If you receive training during 1999 and are willing to share your experiences please contact David Hassell at BECTa, Milburn Hill Road, Science Park, Coventry CV4 7JJ; e-mail: david_hassell@becta.org.uk ■

References and further reading

Department for Education and Employment (DfEE) (1997) *Connecting the Learning Society – The Government's consultation paper on the National Grid for Learning*. Can be viewed at: dfee.gov.uk/grid/consult/index.htm

DfEE (1998a) *Open for Learning, Open for Business: The Government's National Grid for Learning challenge*. Can be viewed at: dfee.gov.uk/grid/challenge/index.htm

DfEE (1998b) *Teachers Meeting the Challenge of Change* (Green Paper). London: DfEE.

Teacher Training Agency (1999) *The Use of ICT in Subject Teaching: Expected outcomes for teachers in England, Wales and Northern Ireland*. London: TTA.

> *David Hassell is the Chair of the GA IT Working Group and works at BECTa in the schools directorate. E-mail: david_hassell@becta.org.uk*

Resources

Sources and websites

> The following contact points and websites are those used within the articles. All website addresses must be prefixed with http://

BECTa

As the lead government agency for ICT and education, BECTa fulfils a key role in supporting the government's initiatives. BECTa works to connect these initiatives with the needs of the educational institutions, teachers and learners across the system. BECTa is a relatively small organisation, but is able to encompass the broad range of educational and ICT developments. BECTa's remit is to ensure that technology supports the DfEE's drive to raise educational standards, and in particular to provide the professional expertise required to support the future development of the National Grid for Learning (*www.ngfl.gov.uk*) and the Virtual Teacher Centre (*vtc.ngfl.gov.uk*).

BECTa has a responsibility for work across the school and further education sectors and manages the Further Education for Learning Resources website which provides a wide range of information and case studies on the use of information technology in further education, including GNVQ: *ferl.becta.org.uk*

In the schools area BECTa is responsible for a range of activities including:
- the accreditation of Managed Services providers (*managedservices.ngfl.gov.uk/explorer.html*)
- developing an effective dialogue with producers of educational software
- investigation of the pedagogy of whole-class computer technologies

The BECTa website provides information on all its activities (*www.becta.org.uk*).

CD-ROMs

Reviews of CD-ROMs can be accessed through the Geography and IT Project NGfL website: *vtc.ngfl.gov.uk/resource/cits/geog*. Look in the 'Software reviews' section of *Teaching Geography*; or the 'Computer update' section of *TES*.

Digital cameras

Actiontec (01782 753355); Adobe (020 8606 4001); Agfa (020 8231 4200, *www.agfahome.com/ephoto*); Canon (0121 680 8062, *www.canon.co.uk/*); Casio (020 8450 9131, *www.casio.com/html/products/cproducts.html*); Epson (01442 261144, *www.epson.co.uk*); Fujifilm (020 7586 5900, *www.fujifilm.com/home/sbu/electi mg/ei_consu.htm*); Hewlett Packard (0118 969 6622, *www.photosmart.com/products/products.html*); JVC (020 8207 7654, *www.jvc-europe.com/*); Kodak (0800 281487, *www.kodak.com/cgi®bin/webCatalog.pl?category=Digital+Cameras*); MicroGrafx (01483 747526); MetaCreations (01756 704000); Nikon (020 8541 4440, *www.nikon.co.uk/eid/index.htm*); Olympus (0800 072 0070, *www.olympusamerica.com*); Panasonic (0990 357357, *www.panasonic.co.uk/*); Ricoh (01782 753355, *www.ricoh®cameras.co.uk/digital/index.html*); Sanyo (01923 477302, *www.sanyo.co.uk/*); Sony (01635 869500, *www.sony.com/*); Vivitar (01793 544829, *www.vivitar.co.uk/digital/index.html*).

Earthquakes and volcanoes

Websites and information on the Kobe earthquake can be found by simply typing 'Kobe' into a search engine. For example: *www.std.kobe-u.ac.jp/newsnet/Eng/quake*; *www.eqc.com/publications/Kobe* and *www.city.Kobe.jp/cityoffice/15/020/quake*

Educational

Australia: Geography Teachers Association of Victoria (*www.netspace.net/au/gtav*).
BBC (*www.bbc.co.uk/education-webguide/pkg_main.p_home*) includes short reviews on educational websites.
Brazil: Bem-Vindo Ao Brasil (*darkwing.uoregon.edu/~sergiok/brasil*).
CTI Centre for Geography, Geology and Meteorology (*www.le.ac.uk/cti*).
Department for Education and Employment (*dfee.gov.uk*)
Chris Durbin is developing a website (for Staffordshire) which contains many useful links for geography teachers (*www.sln.org.uk/geography*).
Geographical Association (*www.geography.org.uk*).
National Grid for Learning (*ngfl.gov.uk*) and Virtual Teacher Centre (*vtc.ngfl.gov.uk*).

Electronic display/presentation

Look on the BECTa website for information on the use of electronic display/presentation in the classroom (*www.becta.org.uk/info-sheets/display.html*). Reviews and information on products is also available at:
Personal Computer World: *www.pcw.co.uk/*; PC Direct: *www.pcdirect.co.uk/* and Zdnet: *www.zdnet.co.uk/pcmag/labs/1999/04/data_projectors/*.

Presentation packages: PowerPoint Made Simple by Stephen, M. (Made Simple Books, price £8.99), and *Microsoft PowerPoint At A Glance* by Microsoft Press (price £15.49).

Computer-to-television adapters/cables: Betterbox (01908 560200, *www.betterbox.com/*); Fox Direct (0990 744500, *www.foxdirect.co.uk/*); Hills Components (01923 424344); Insight (0800 706 0510, *www.insight.com/*); Misco (01933 400400, *www.misco.co.uk/*).

Interactive whiteboards: Accurate (0113 250 0500, www.accurate.plc.uk/); Matrix (0800 980 9864, *www.matrixdisplay.com/*); Promethean (01254 676921, *www.promethean.co.uk/*); Vupoint (01438 716564, *www.vupoint.co.uk/*).

LCD panels: Misco, Pico Direct (0870 729 6097, *www.picodirect.co.uk/*); Presentation Direct (0800 174164); Presentations by Design (020 8450 3488).

Large screen monitors: Atomwide (01689 814500, *www.atomwide.co.uk/*).

Plasma displays: Tech Direct (020 8286 2222, *www.techdirect.co.uk*); W2.FM Direct (0118 973 0855, *www.w2fm.co.uk/*).

Projectors: Accurate, Boxlight (01732 840404, *www.boxlight.com/*); Just Projectors (07000 587877, *www.projectors.co.uk/*); Matrix, Pico Direct, Presentation Direct, Tech Direct, Vupoint, W2.FM Direct.

Fieldwork

Virtual fieldwork has yet to develop 'live' websites, but one that may be of is: *www.stromboli.ch*. Search the Net for 'webcams' (video cameras linked live to a website) and use them for virtual fieldwork.

GIS

AEGIS2 Advisory Unit: Computers in Education (01707 266174, fax: 01707 273684, *www.advisory-unit.org.uk*); *ArcView* Environmental Science Research Institute (01923 210450, fax: 01923 210739, *www.esriuk.com*); *ATLAS Map Maker* Adept Scientific (01462 480055); *Excel (version 7 onwards)* (*www.microsoft.com/uk/education/*); *Idrisi* The Idrisi Project (00 1 508 793 7526, fax: 00 1 508 793 8842, *www.clarklabs.org/*); *MapInfo Professional* (01753 848200, e-mail: uk@mapinfo.com, *www.mapinfo.com/software/index.html*); *Ordnance Survey* (023 8079 2906, *www.ordsvy.gov.uk/home/index.html*); *SCAMP* (01273 483890, fax: 01273 479645, *www.pebbleshore.co.uk/*).

Leisure and tourism

Places to start searching include: *www.yahoo.co.uk* and Henley College: *www.henleycol.ac.uk*.

Crossing to the Continent: Hoverspeed (*www.hoverspeed.co.uk*); P&O (*www.poef.com*); Scandinavian Seaways (*www.scansea.com*); Eurostar (*www.eurostar.com/eurostar/eurostar.html*).

Leisure: Birmingham City Council (*birmingham.gov.uk*)

Tourist Boards/virtual tours: ABTA (*www.abtanet.com*); Brazil (*www.brazil.org.uk*); British Tourist Authority (*www.bta.org.uk*); Manchester (*www.u-net.com/manchester*) ; New York (*www.totalny.com*); Rough Guides (*roughguides.com*); SE England Tourist Board (*www.seetb.org.uk*); The virtual tourist (*www.vtourist.com*); Welsh Tourist Board (*www.tourism.wales.gov.uk*).

Travel: British Rail (*www.railtrack.co.uk/ travel*); National Express (*www.nationalexpress.co.uk*)